Oakville Ontario in Colour Photos, Saving Our History One Photo at a Time

Photography
by Barbara Raué
2014

Series Name:
Cruising Ontario

Book 94: Oakville

Cover Photo: 1856 Custom House and Bank of Toronto on the Erchless Estate – now part of Oakville Museum

Series Name: Cruising Ontario
Saving Our History One Photo at a Time
in colour photos

Other Books by Barbara Raue

Coins of Gold

Arrows, Indians and Love

The Life and Times of Barbara
Volume 1: Inventions That Have Enhanced My Life
Volume 2: Entertainment That I Have Enjoyed
Volume 3: East Coast Trips
Volume 4: Olympics Have Always Intrigued Me
Volume 5: Wonders of the World
Volume 6: Caribbean Cruises We Have Enjoyed
Volume 7: Animals
Volume 8: Storms and Other Major Disasters in My Lifetime
Volume 9: Wars, Terrorist Attacks and Major Disasters

The Cromwell Family Book

Laura Secord Discovered

Visit Barbara's website to view all of her books
http://barbararaue.ca

Many of the Ojibwa who moved into southern Ontario (1701-1800) came to be known as the Mississauga. They were primarily hunter-gatherers who travelled in small bands. In winter they hunted in the interior and in the warmer months they came to the mouths of the rivers and creeks flowing into the Great Lakes. The Ojibwa gave Sixteen Mile Creek a name which meant "having two outlets" because of the gravel bar dividing its mouth. Here they fished for salmon.

Under the Royal Proclamation of 1763, European settlement could not proceed without a formal treaty with the aboriginal proprietors of the land. In 1805 the Mississauga agreed to surrender all the lands from Etobicoke River to Burlington Bay. Since the fishery was important to them, the Mississauga insisted on reserving for themselves the lower portions of the rivers, including Sixteen Mile Creek, together with the flood plains where they had their camps and small cornfields. These reserved parcels were ceded to the Crown in 1820. The Mississauga moved out of the area in 1847. Their descendants now live at the New Credit Reserve near Hagersville, Ontario.

Oakville is situated on Lake Ontario in southern Ontario. In 1793, Dundas Street was surveyed for a military road. By 1807, British immigrants settled the area around Dundas Street and on the shores of Lake Ontario.

In 1827, George Chalmers built a settlement with water-powered mills beside the Sixteen at the Dundas crossing. A small sawmill and gristmill were constructed on the valley bottom at the edge of a pond formed by a dam. In future years, a church, school, ashery, blacksmith shop, distillery, and tavern provided services to the local farmers. The village continued to prosper with the addition of a tannery, carding mill and steam stave mill until the coming of the railroad to Oakville in 1855.

William Chisholm, Oakville's founder, was born to United Empire Loyalist parents in Shelburne, Nova Scotia in 1788. After moving to Burlington, Upper Canada, Chisholm fought in the War of 1812, entered politics and tried his hand at farming.

In 1827, William Chisholm purchased 960 acres of uncleared land at the mouth of Sixteen Mile Creek. He built mills, and laid out the Town of Oakville. He established a shipyard, dredged the mouth of the river and built two piers out into the lake to create a protected harbour. The first ship launched from his shipyard was the eighty foot, two-masted *Trafalgar* with a capacity of 50 tonnes of wheat. His was one of five shipyards on the Sixteen which launched five to ten wooden sailing ships per year during the next three decades. As many as sixteen sailing schooners might be in the harbour at any one time loading up with white oak staves, and wheat destined for Lower Canada, Europe and the United States. In 1863, Oakville's largest ship was launched, the three-masted, two-hundred foot *Monarch* with a capacity of 348 tonnes. Chisholm also launched three steamboats in Oakville – *Constitution, Oakville* and *Burlington*. With 80-horsepower wood-fueled engines driving their paddle wheels, early steamships also needed masts and sails to capture favourable winds. The *Constitution*, launched in 1833, was 150 feet long with berths for 51 passengers. During the 1830s and 1840s she connected Oakville to ports on both sides of the lake.

As the village prospered and grew, roads and ships were built to connect it with the rest of Upper Canada. The area was developed by his son, Robert Kerr Chisholm and his brother-in-law Thomas Merrick.

Water transport moved the region's timber and grain and also its people. The two hour steamboat trip from York to Oakville was faster than the six-hour stagecoach trip and far more comfortable.

Although the bulk of the town and early development was on the east bank of the Sixteen, from the start the major industries were located on the west side. It was usual for the workers in the shipyards, brewery, sawmill, and tannery to live there too. Oakville's first industries included shipbuilding, timber shipment, and wheat farming. The town became industrialized with the opening of oil refineries, and Procor (manufactured railway shipping cars), and the establishment of the Ford Motor Company's Canadian headquarters and plant.

Trafalgar Township settlers lived in isolation in the early years. Travel was difficult and there was no newspaper or postal service. The first stagecoach service began along Dundas Street in the 1820s. By 1833, stagecoaches were also travelling along Lakeshore Road, and Oakville had regular steamship service to Hamilton and York.

Farmers north of Oakville needed a road to deliver their crops to Oakville's mills and harbour. In 1831 the House of Assembly provided funds for the construction of Seventh Line or Trafalgar Road. Fifteen years later this road was upgraded to a planked road complete with toll booths.

With postal service beginning in 1822 and a newspaper (the Oakville Observer) starting up in 1836, Oakville and Trafalgar Townships early years of isolation came to an end.

By the 1870s Oakville was becoming a year-round resort town. In summer hotels were filled to capacity and hundreds more arrived on day excursions via steamer. Tourists could rent canoes, rowboats, and sailboats. The town's waterfront beach offered swimming and fishing.

At the end of the 19th century Oakville began to attract wealthy summer residents. Farm fields bordering the lake were developed into large waterfront properties with luxurious residents and landscaped gardens. Some of Canada's best-known horses were bred at these estates.

Beginning in the 1870s, sailing for pleasure and competition expanded greatly on Lake Ontario. Oakville became a destination for Royal Canadian Yacht Club Races from Toronto. On summer weekends, fifty or more yachts were often tied up in the harbour. Oakville's shipbuilders turned their attention to pleasure craft. Captain James Andrew built the yacht *Canada* at his shipyard in 1896. It won the first Canada-USA match race for sailing yachts. The trophy, known since as "The Canada's Cup", is still competed for one hundred years later.

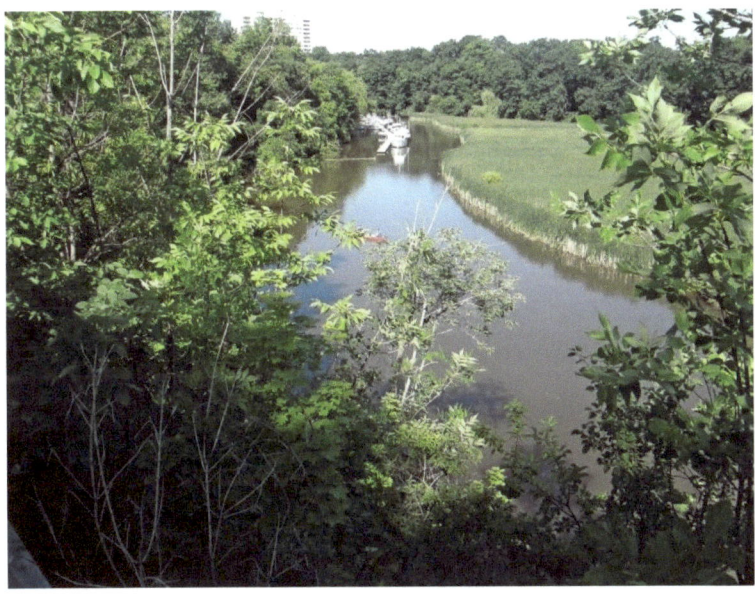

Index

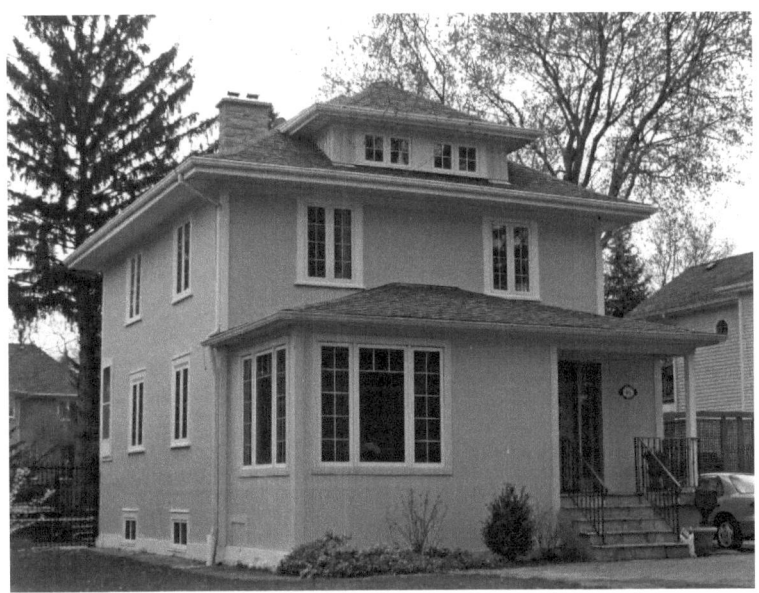

46 Burnet Street – Italianate, dormer in attic

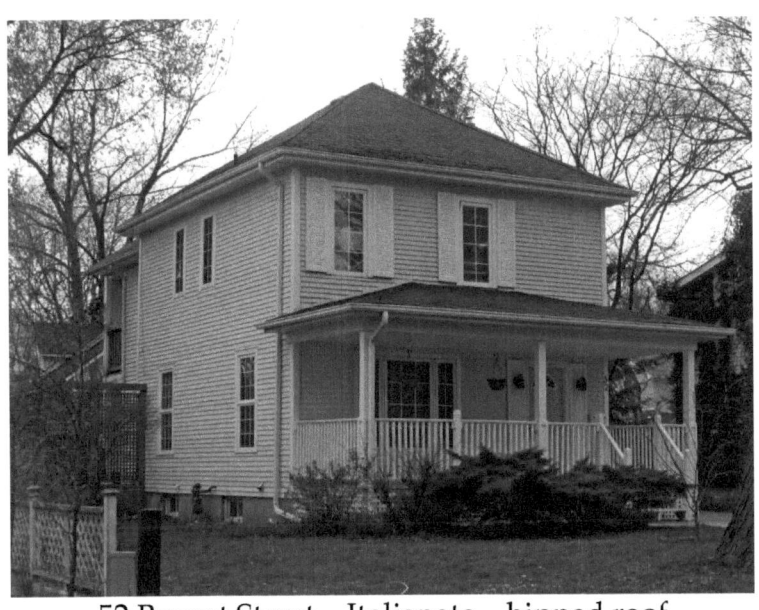

52 Burnet Street – Italianate – hipped roof

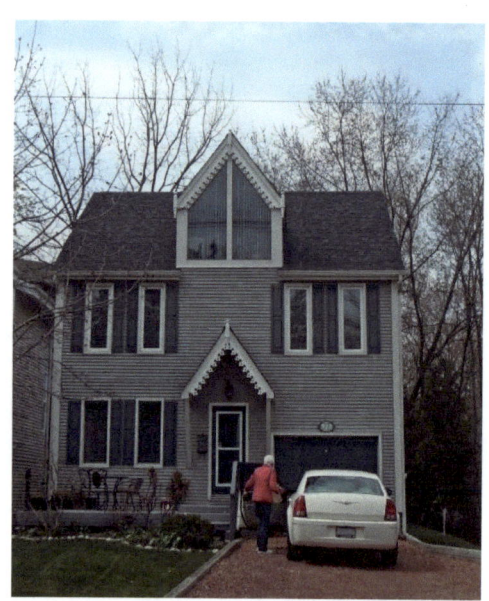

77 Burnet Street

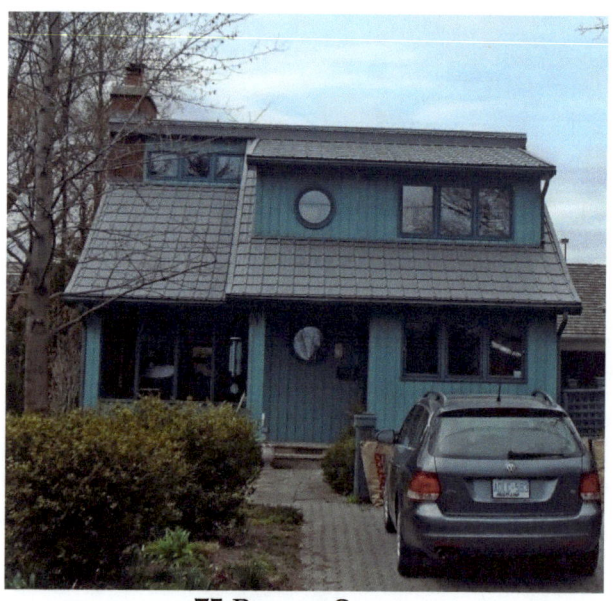

75 Burnet Street

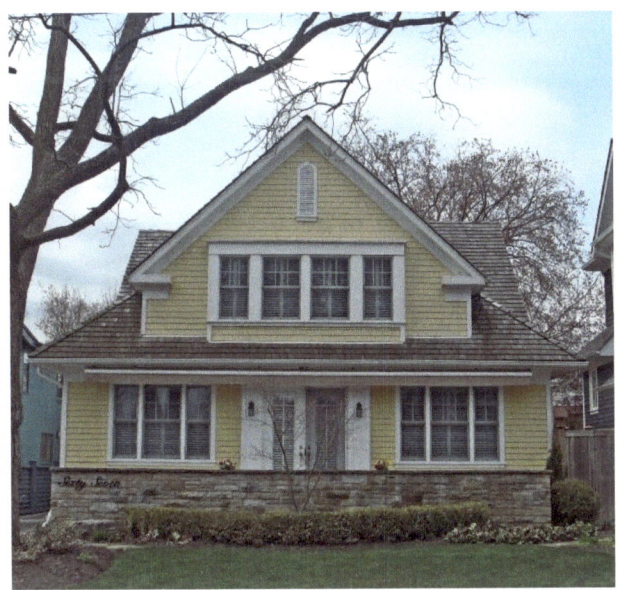

67 Burnet Street

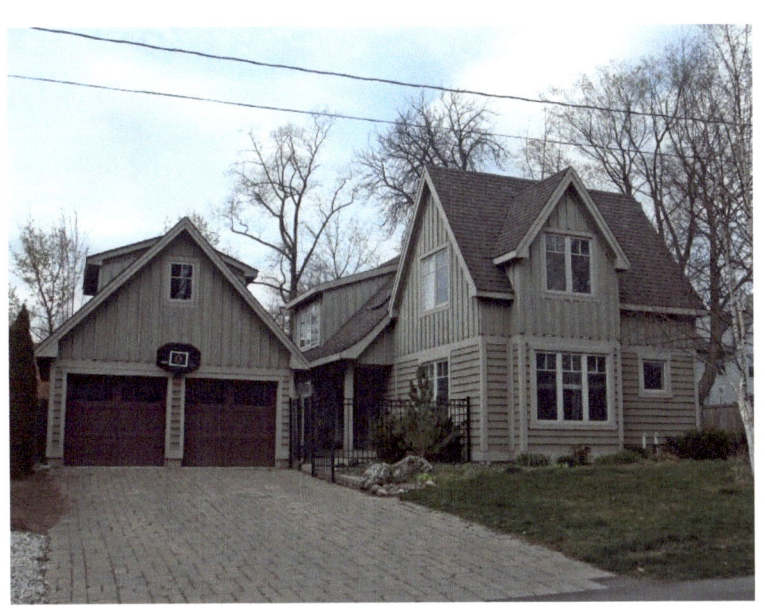

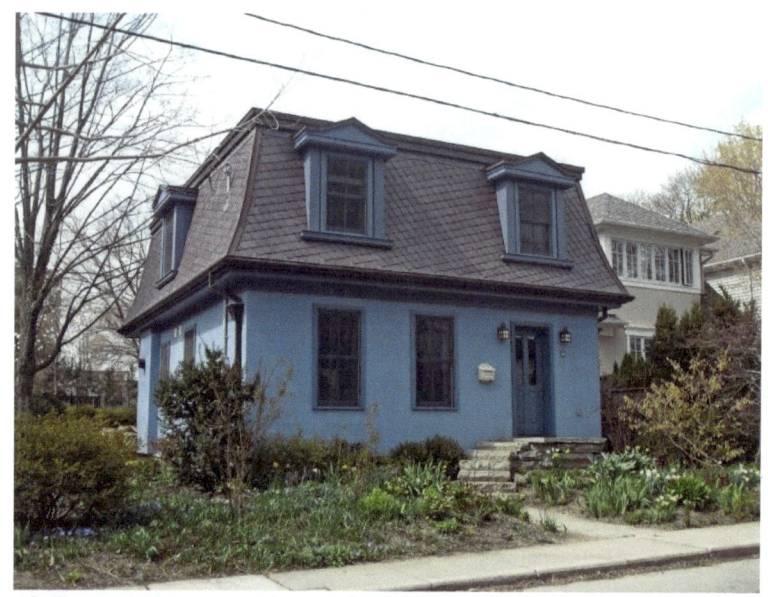

43 Burnet Street – Second Empire style - mansard roof, dormers

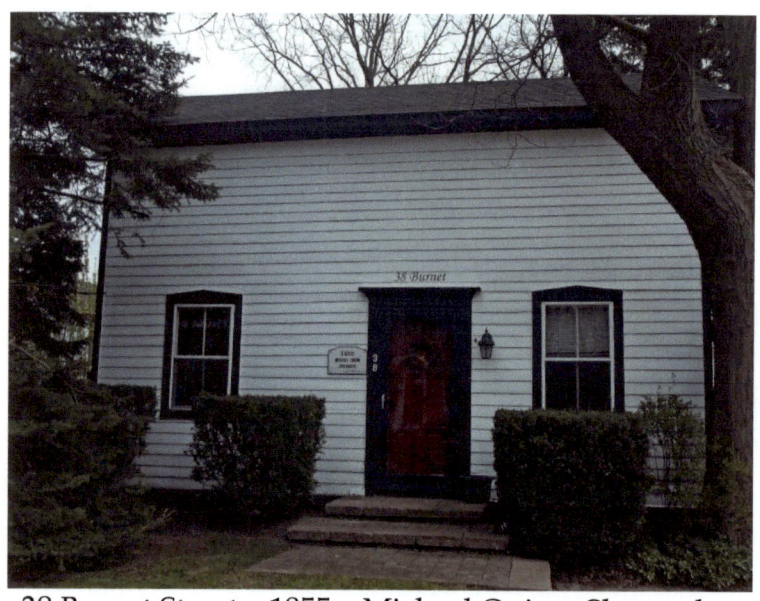

38 Burnet Street – 1855 – Michael Quinn, Shoemaker

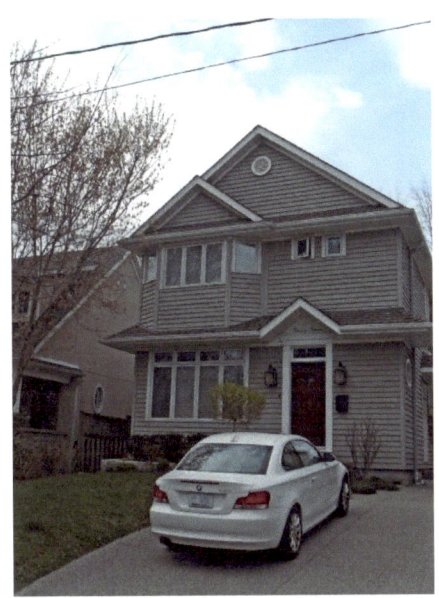

37 Burnet Street

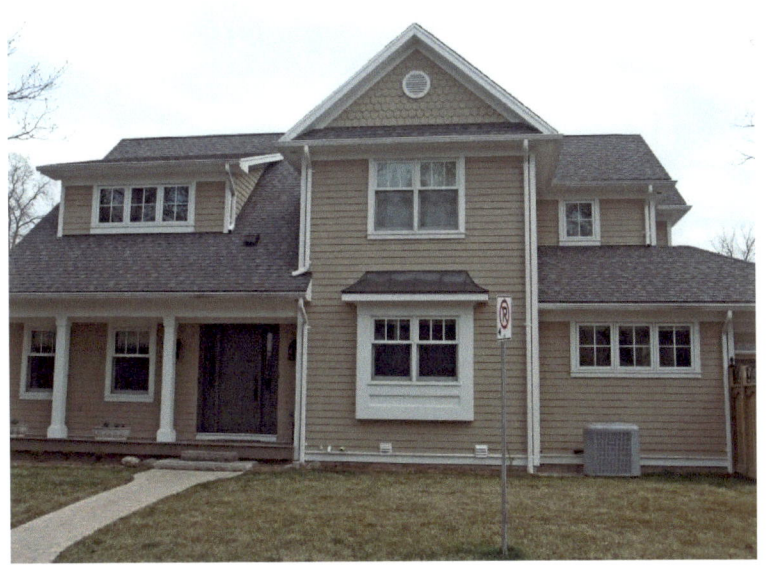

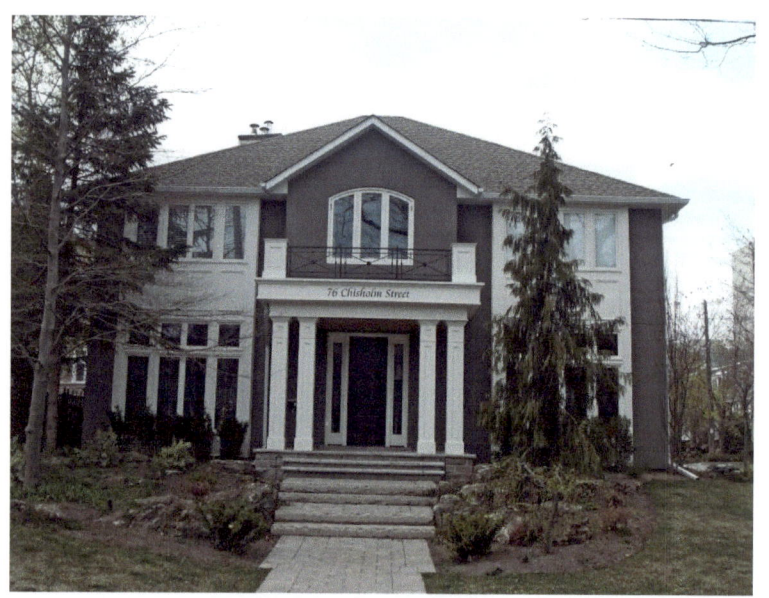

76 Chisholm Street

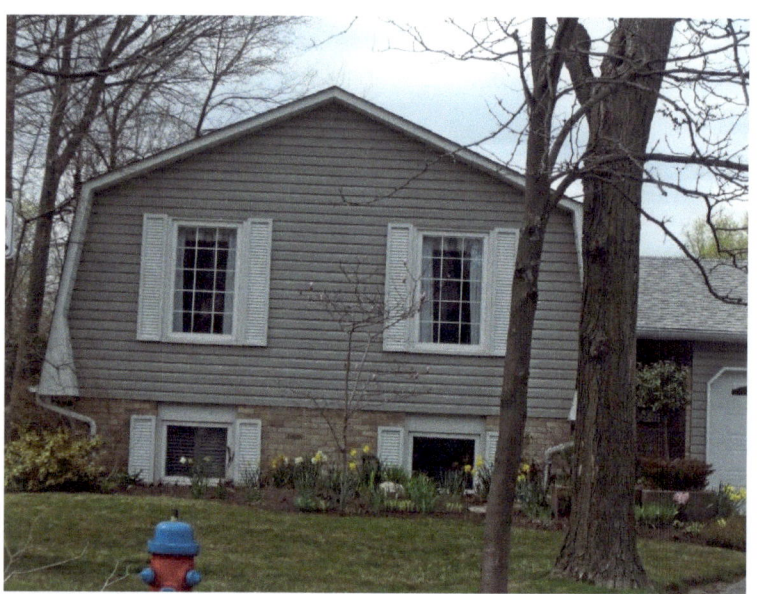

Gothic Revival

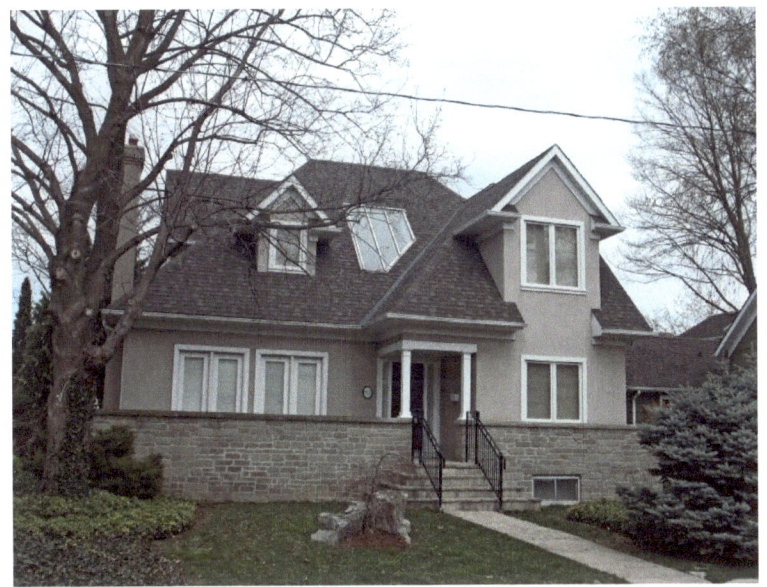

63 Chisholm Street

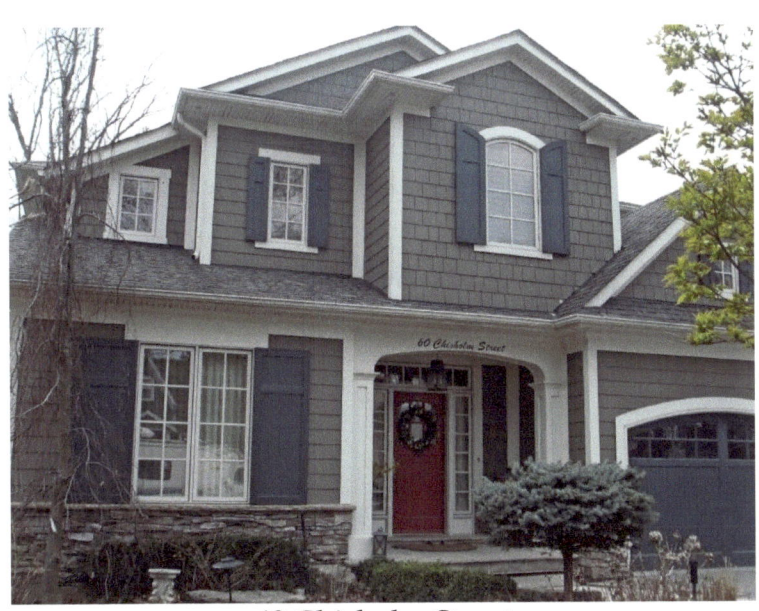

60 Chisholm Street

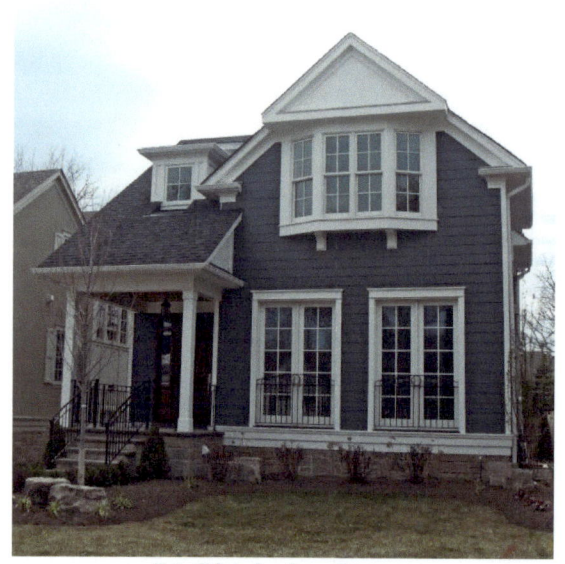

54 Chisholm Street

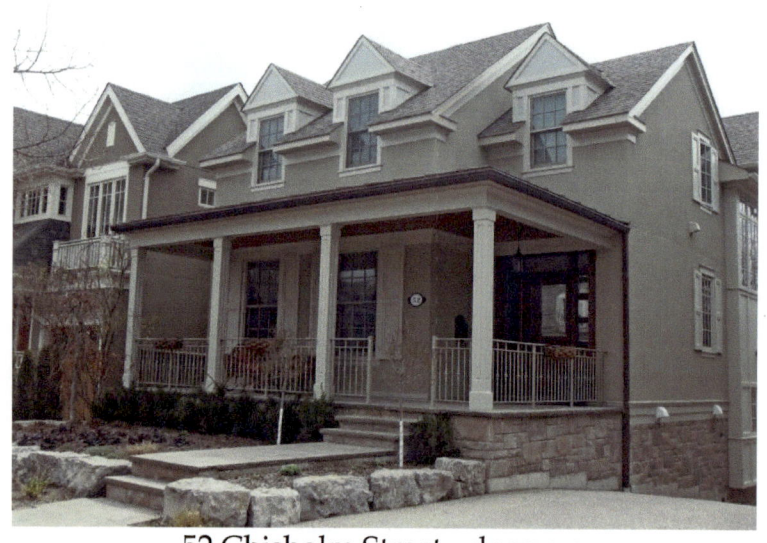

52 Chisholm Street - dormers

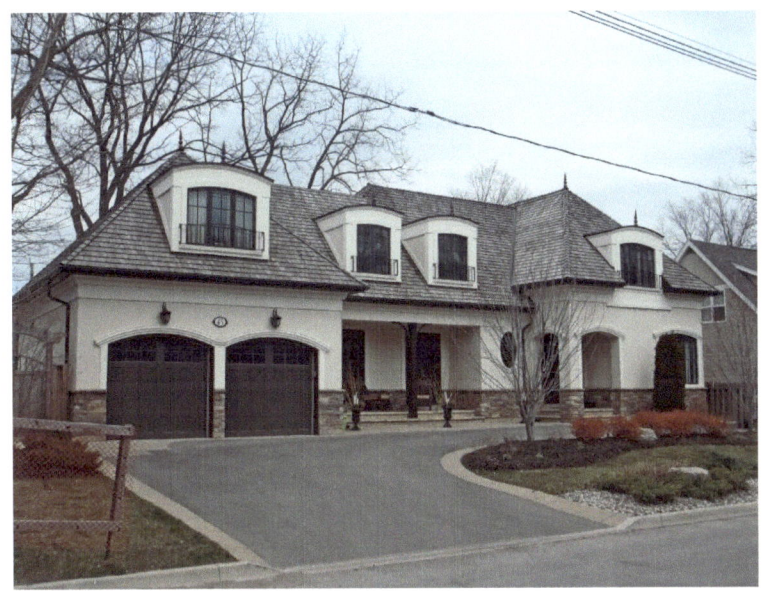

45 Chisholm Street

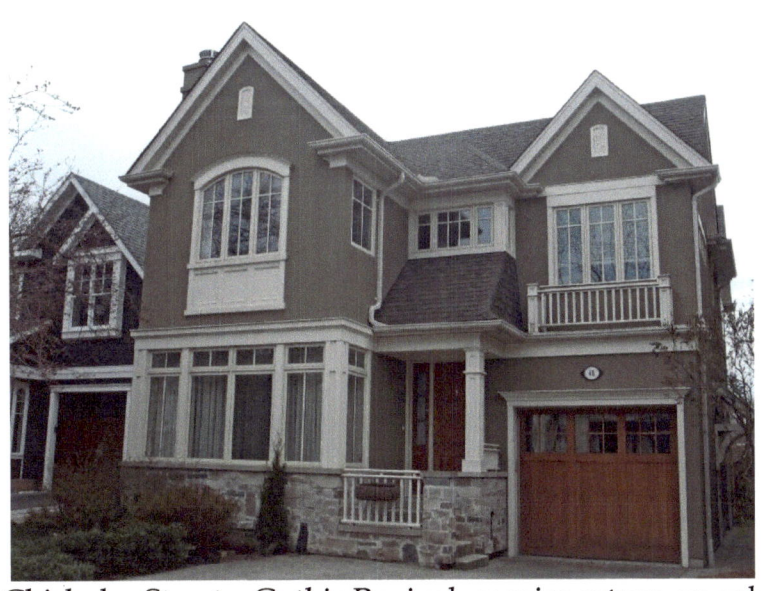

48 Chisholm Street – Gothic Revival, cornice return on gables

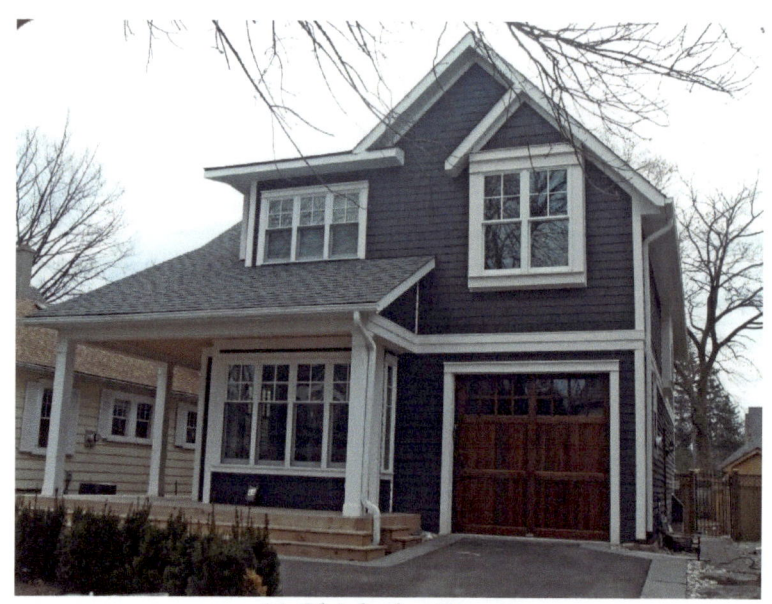

44 Chisholm Street

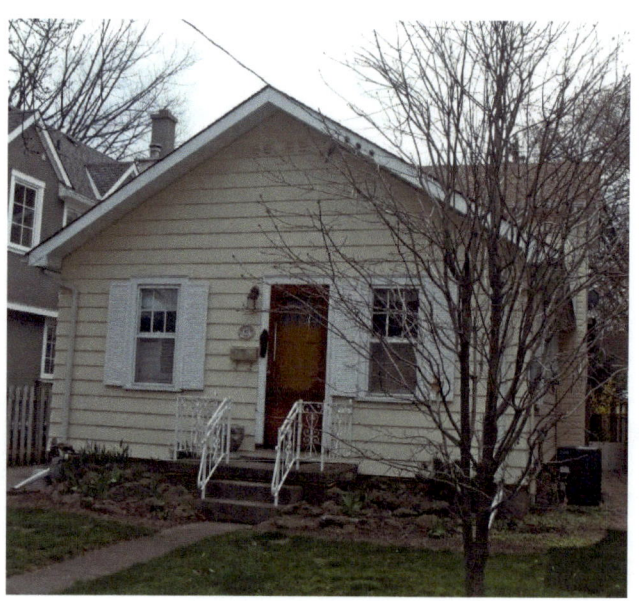

40 Chisholm Street

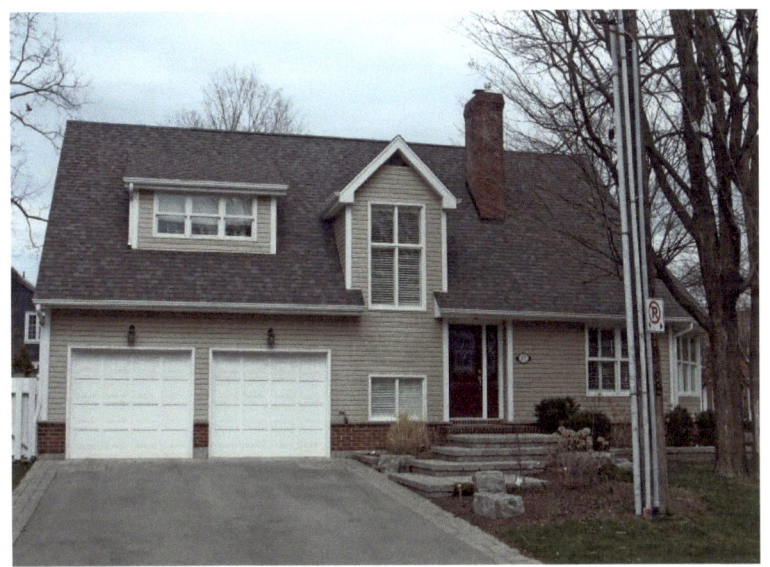

37 Chisholm Street

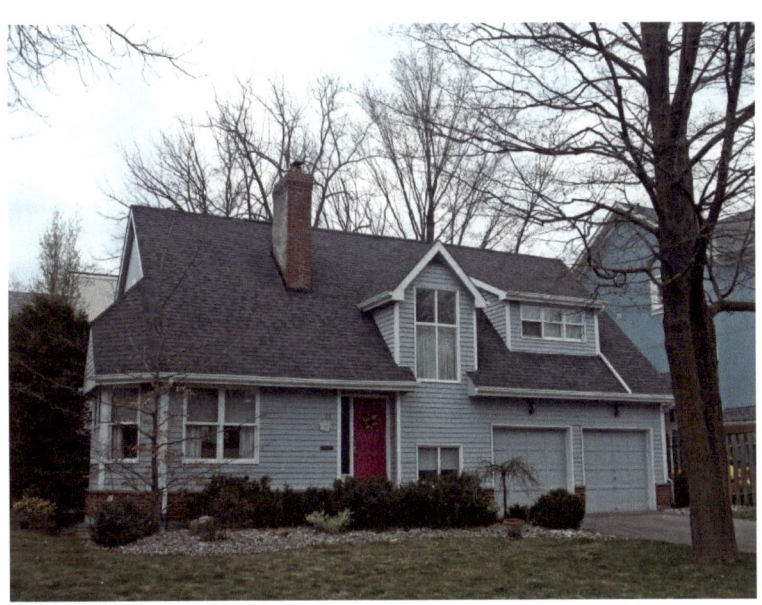

#11

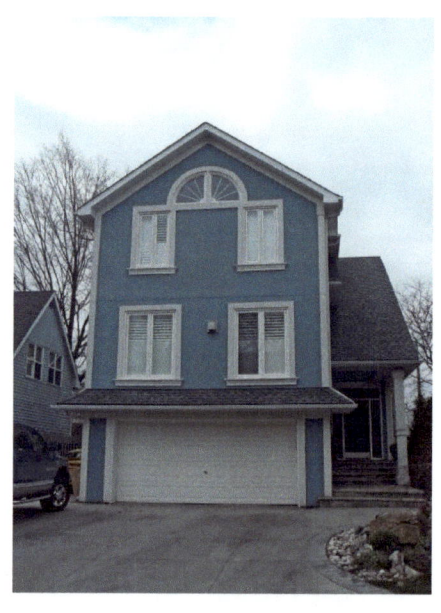

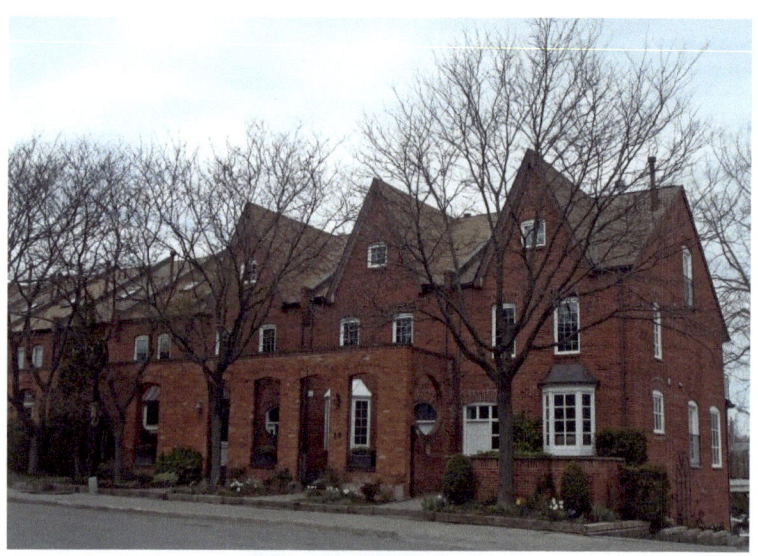

#39 – Gothic Revival

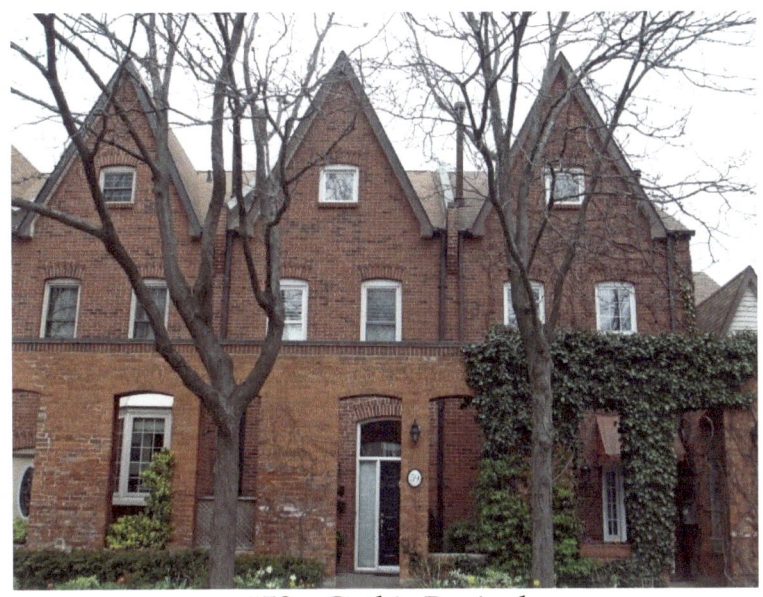

#59 – Gothic Revival

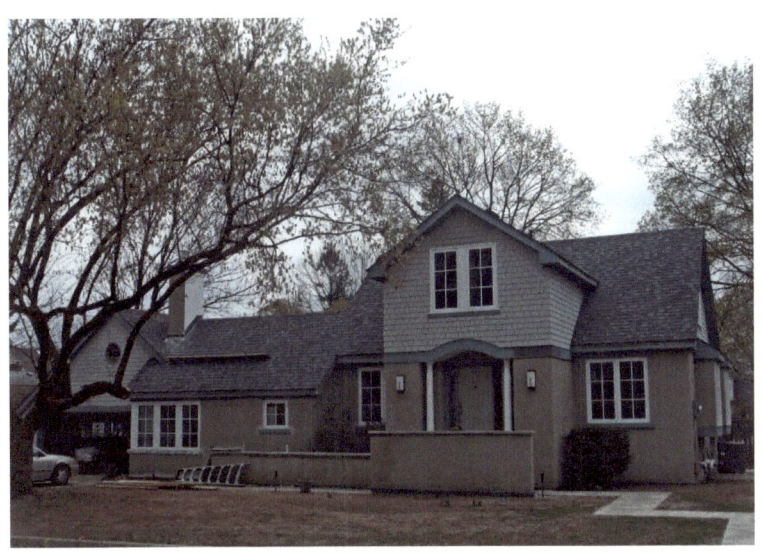

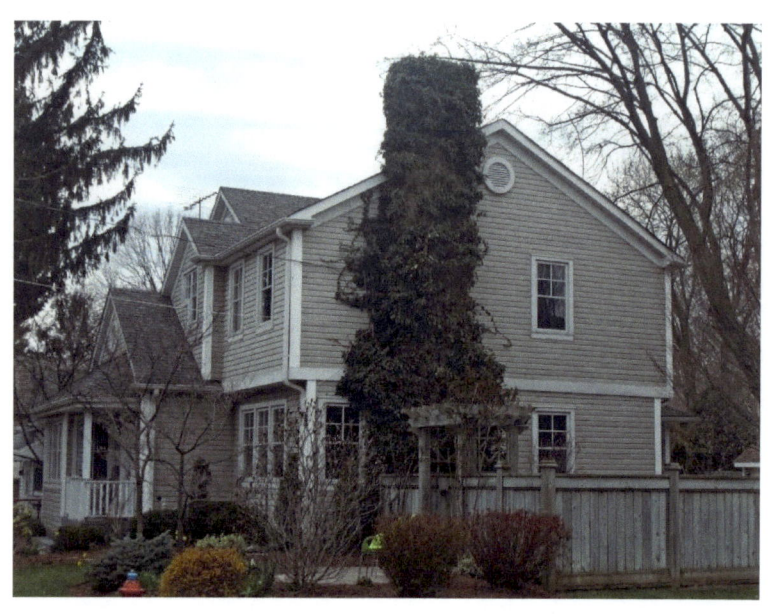

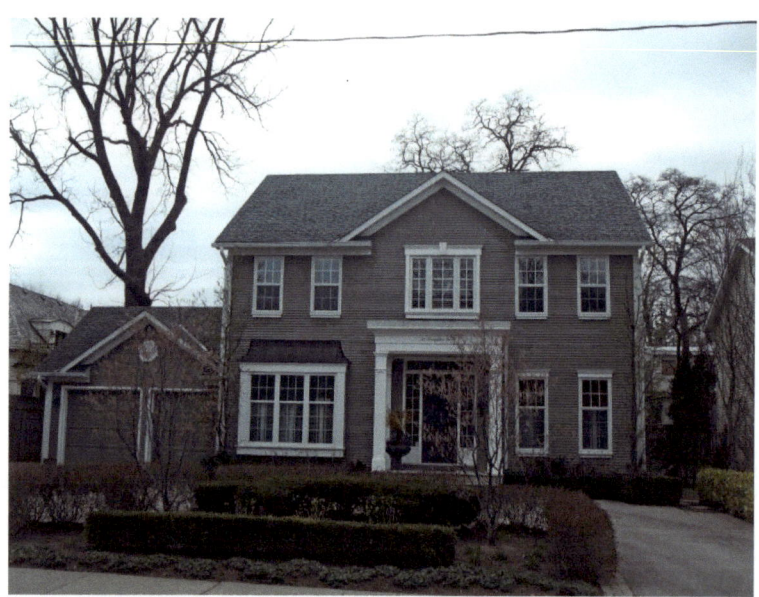

50 Forsythe Street – cornice return on gables

Oakville Museum

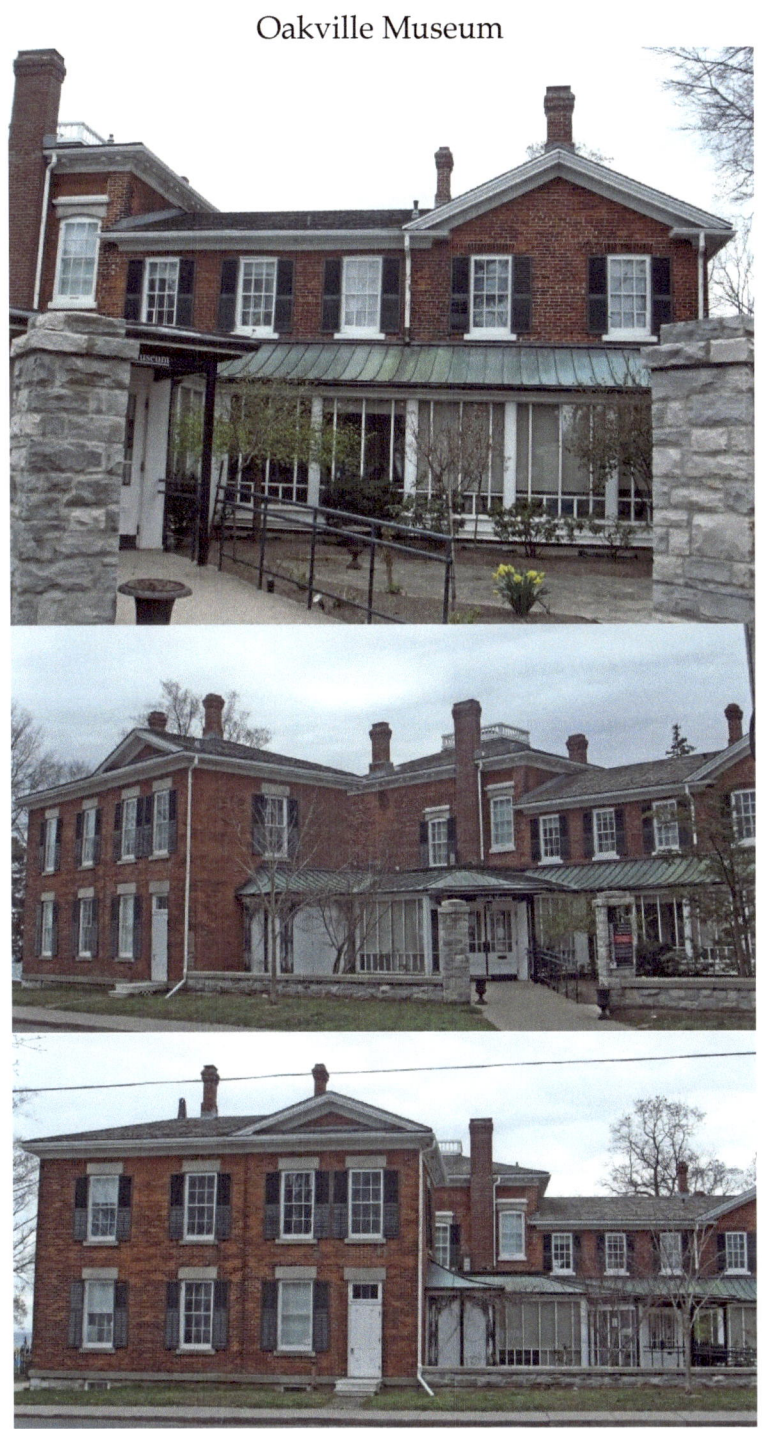

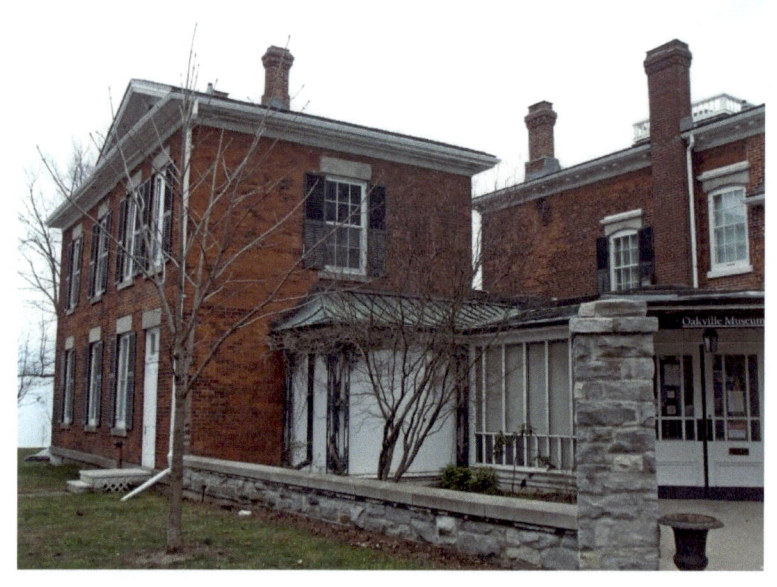

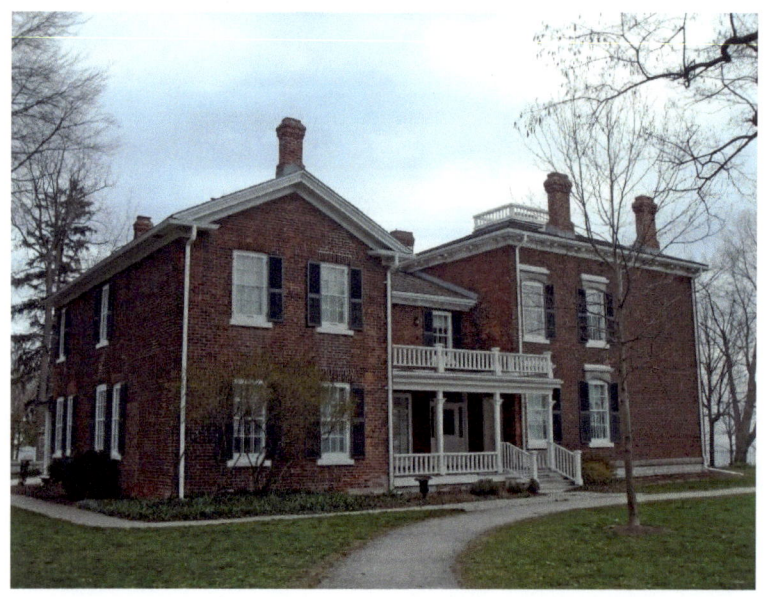

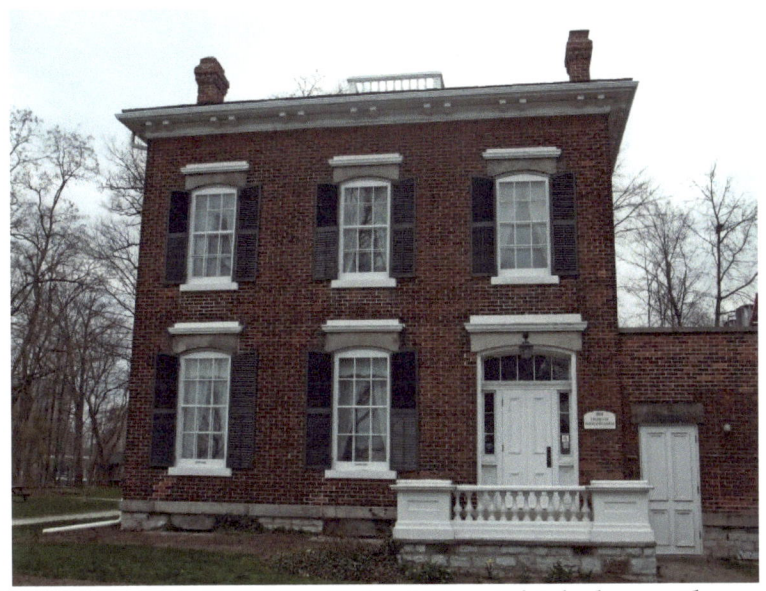

Erchless built in 1858 by Robert Kerr Chisholm on the east
bank of the harbour mouth

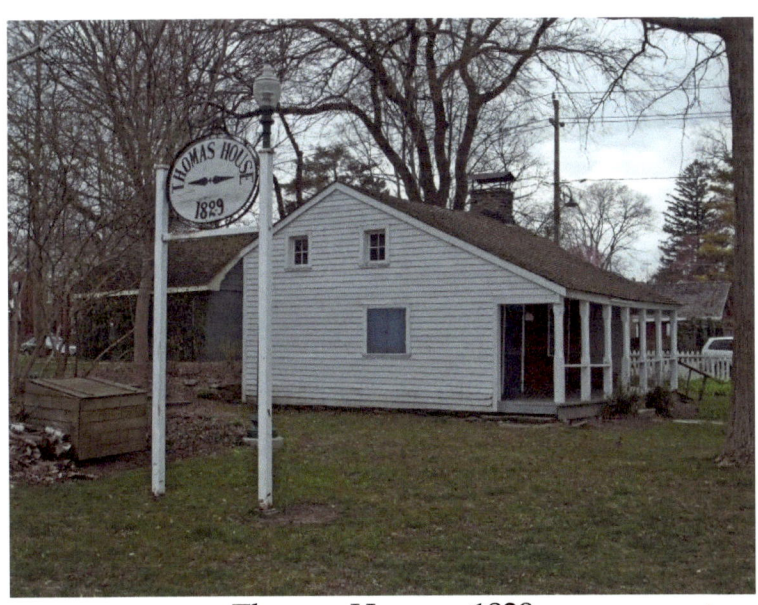

Thomas House – 1829
The original home of the Merrick Thomas Family

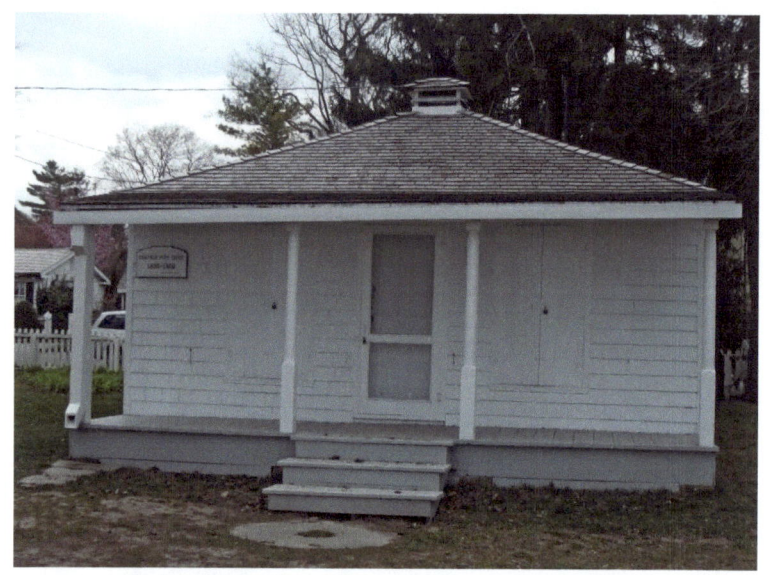

Oakville's First Post Office – 1835-1857

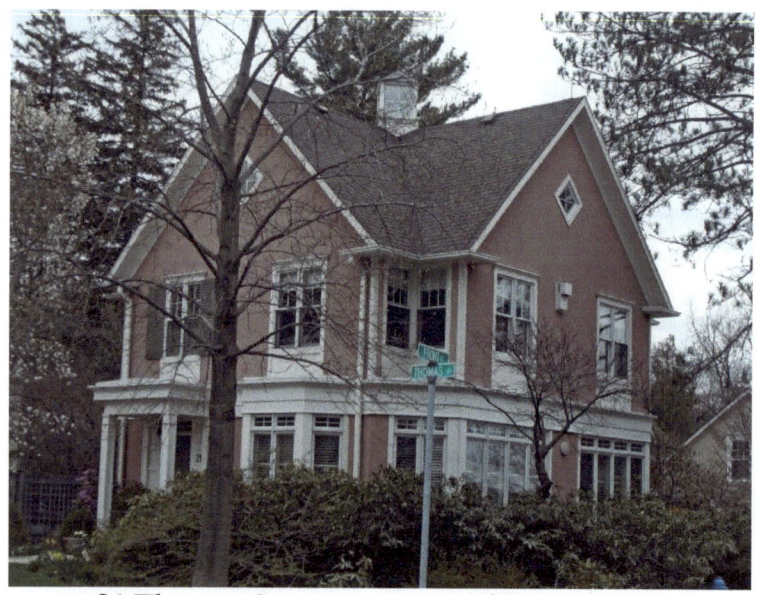

21 Thomas Street at corner of Front Street

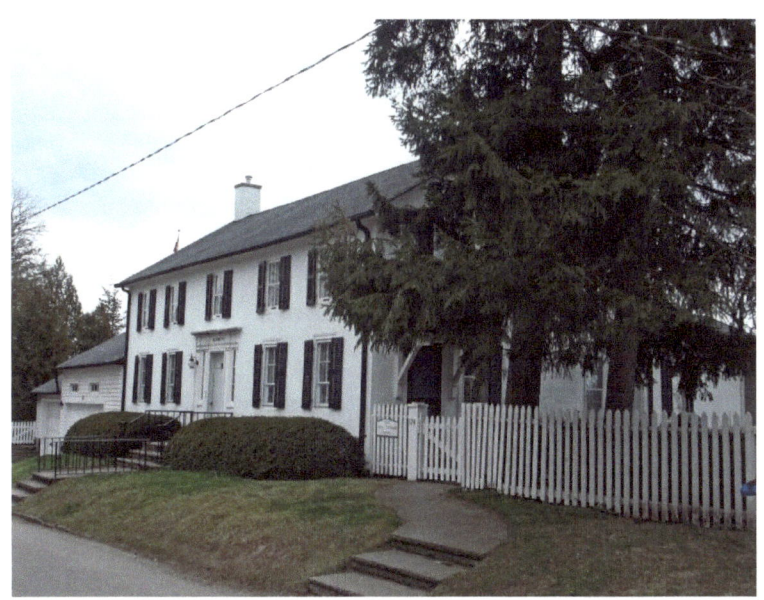

174 Front Street – 1837 – Georgian style
James McDonald, Carpenter

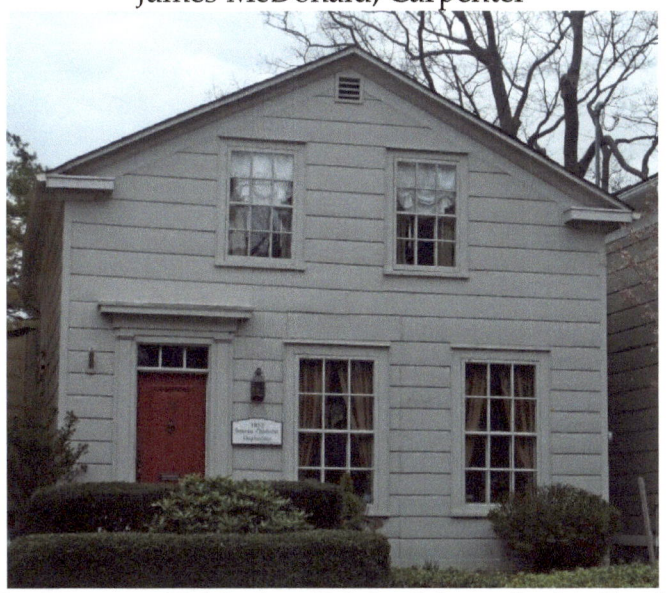

1852 – Duncan Chisholm, Shipbuilder – Gothic Revival,
cornice return on gable

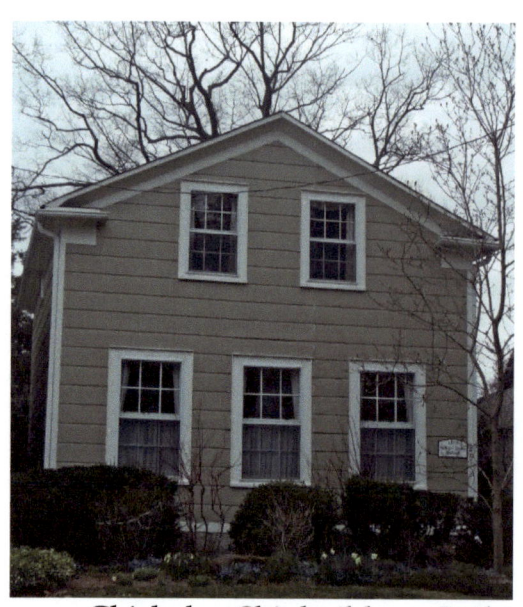

1852 – Duncan Chisholm, Shipbuilder – Gothic Revival, cornice return on gable

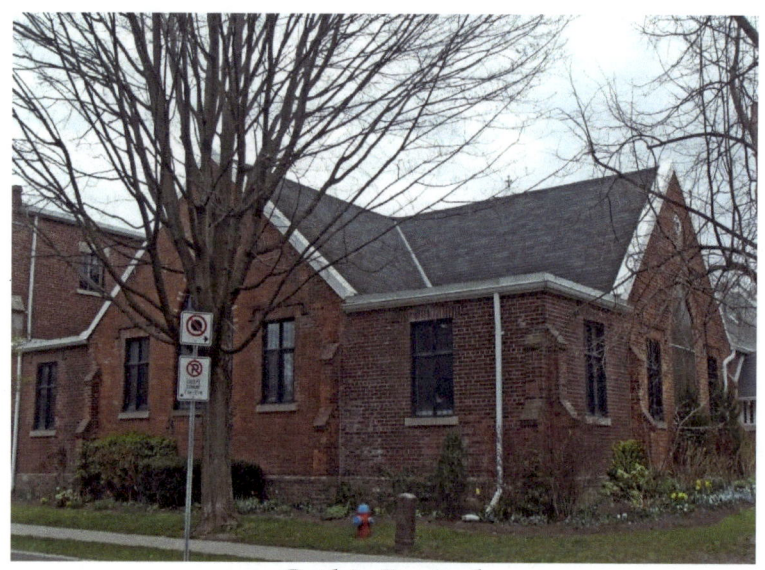

Gothic Revival

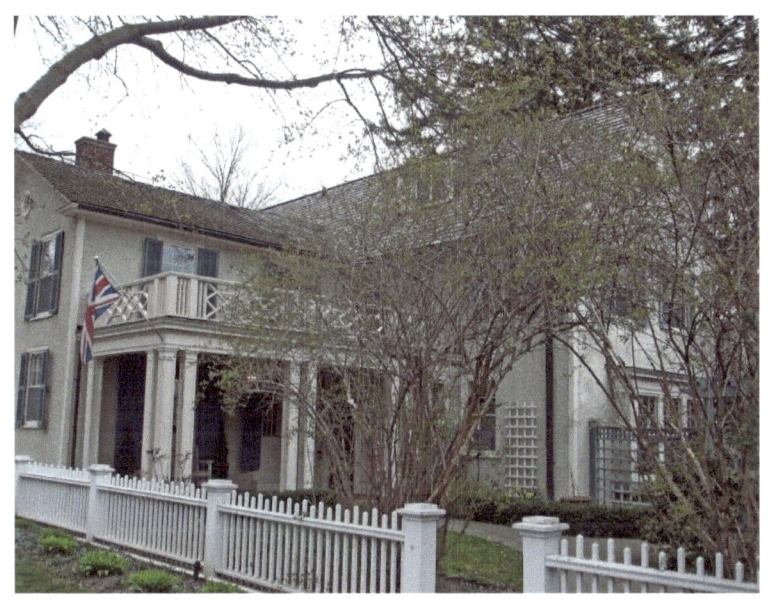

1839 – Captain William Wilson – Gothic Revival
1854 – "Glenorchy" – Peter MacDougald, Grain Merchant,
Mayor of Oakville 1875

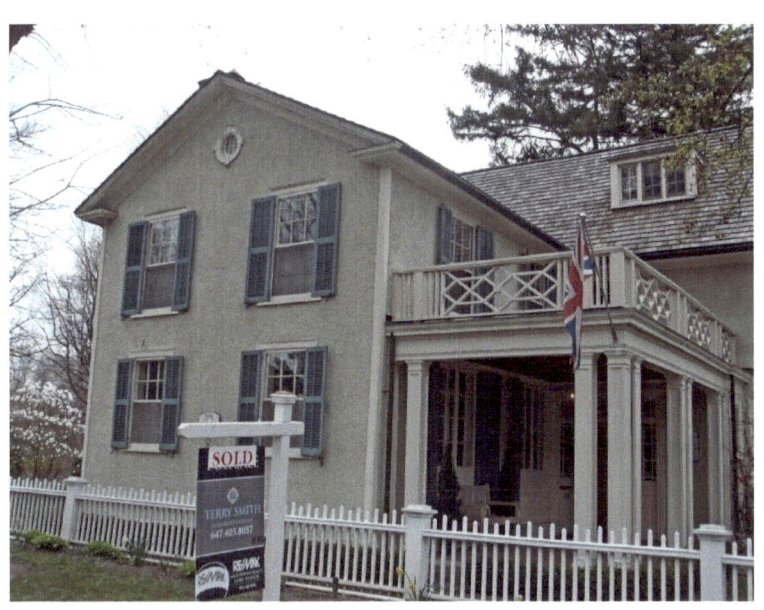

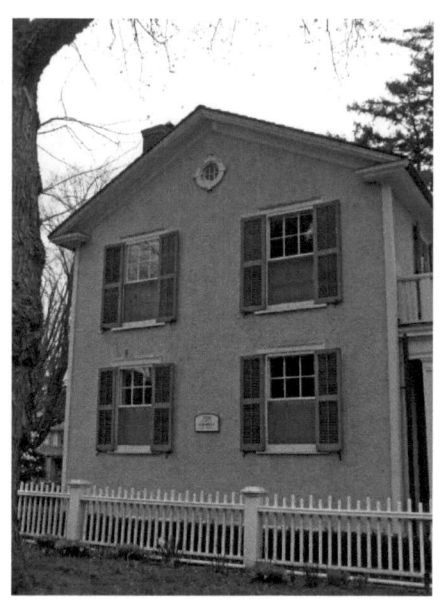

1839 – P. A. MacDougald

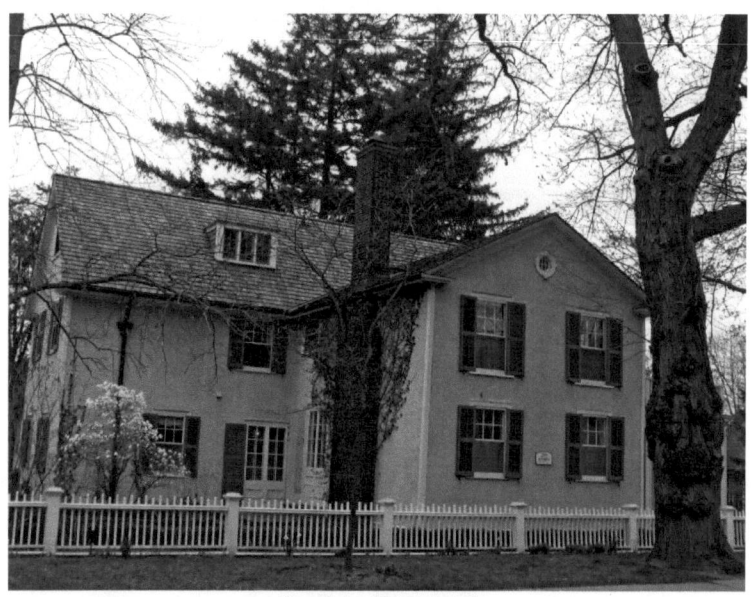

Gothic Revival

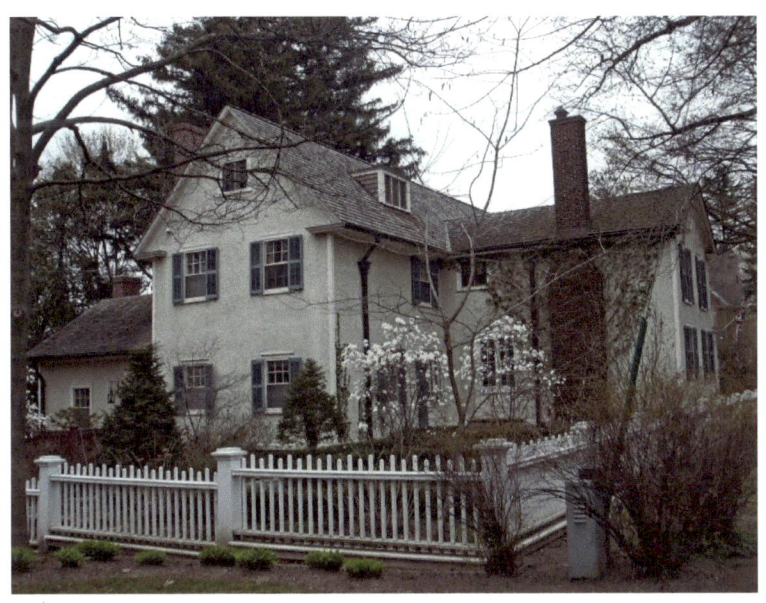

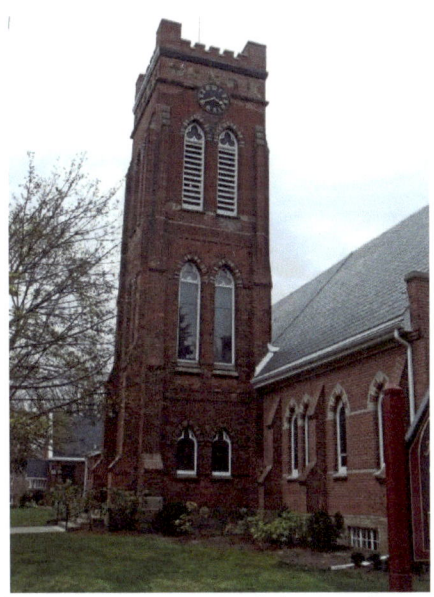

160 William Street - St. Jude's Anglican Church
buttresses, lancet windows

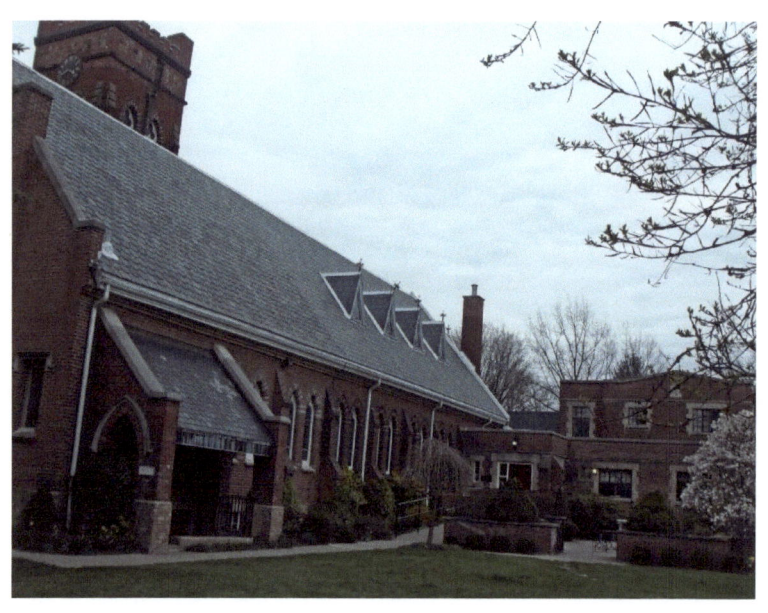

St. Jude's Anglican Church
Founded in 1839, built from 1883

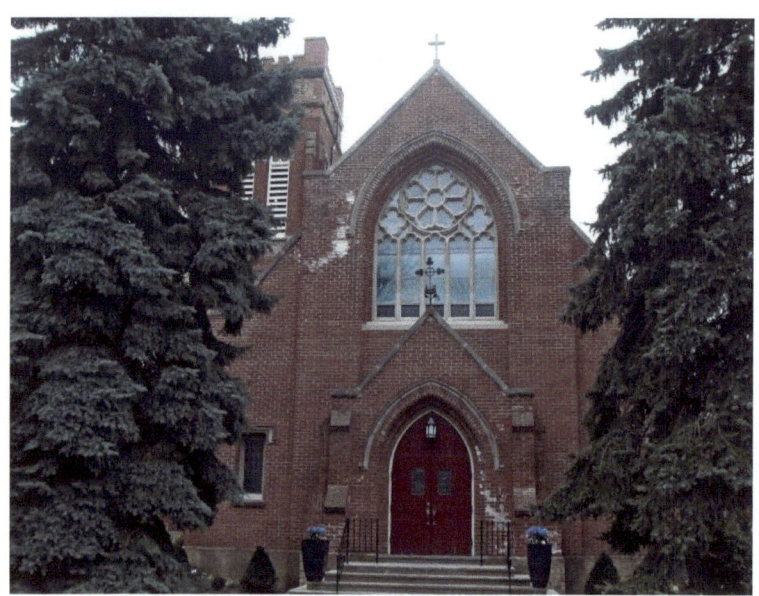

Rose window

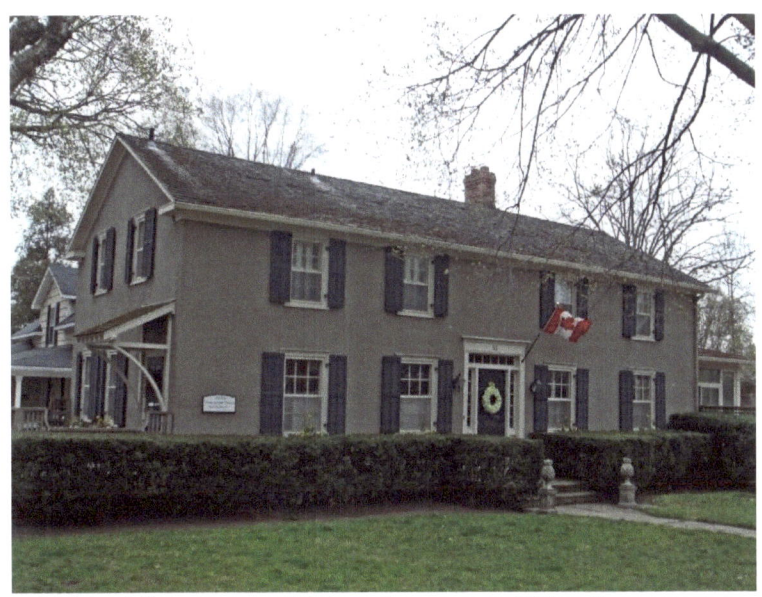

1834 – Thomas and John Sweeney, Ship Carpenters
Georgian style

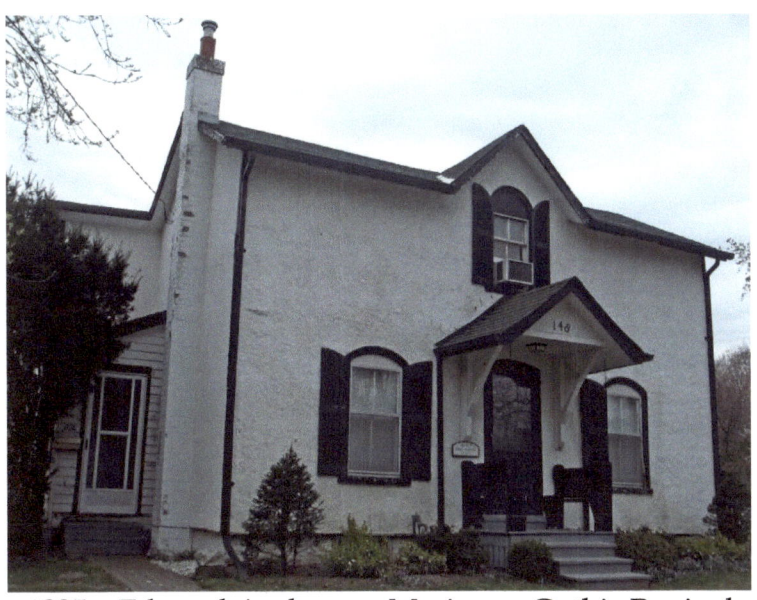

1835 – Edward Anderson, Mariner – Gothic Revival

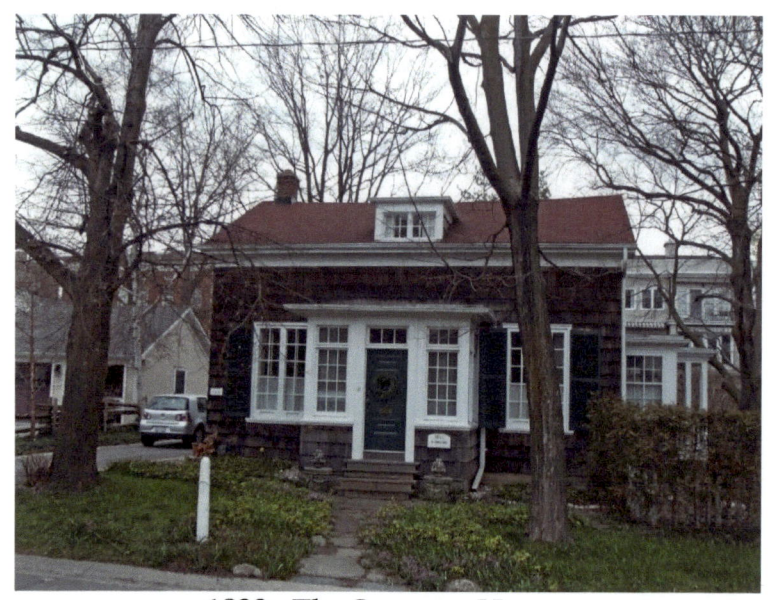

1833 –The Summer House

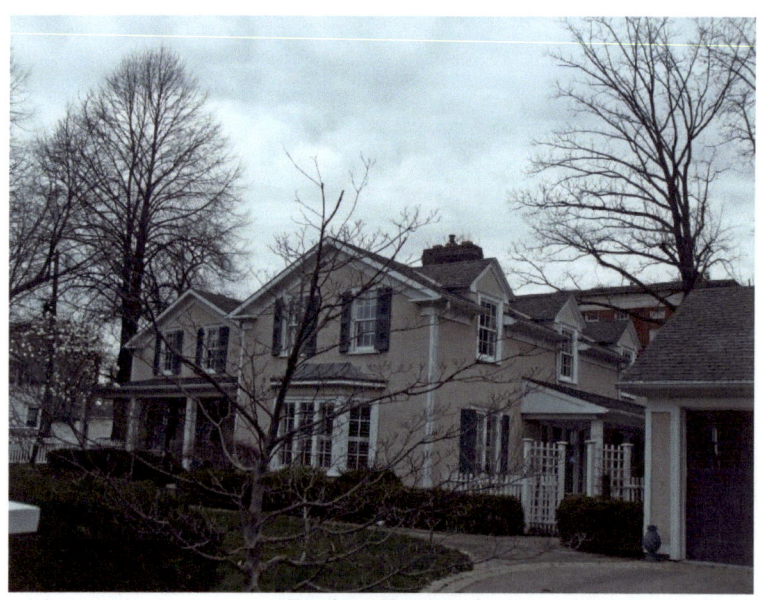

Gothic Revival

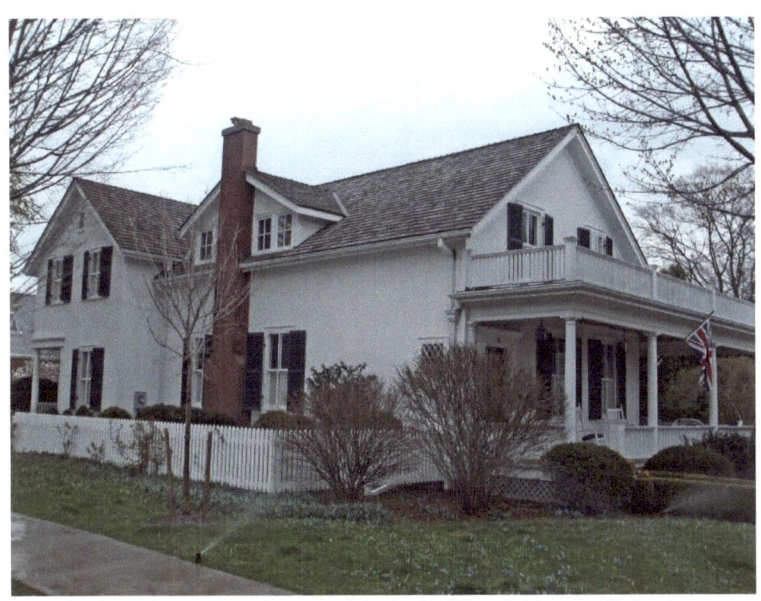

1850 – Captain Samuel McGiffin, Master Mariner
Gothic Revival

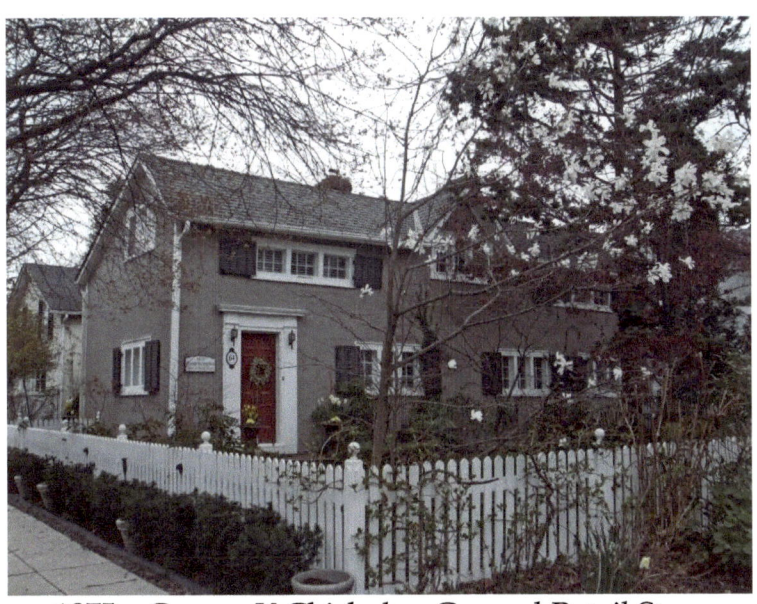

1875 – George K Chisholm, General Retail Store
64 Navy Street

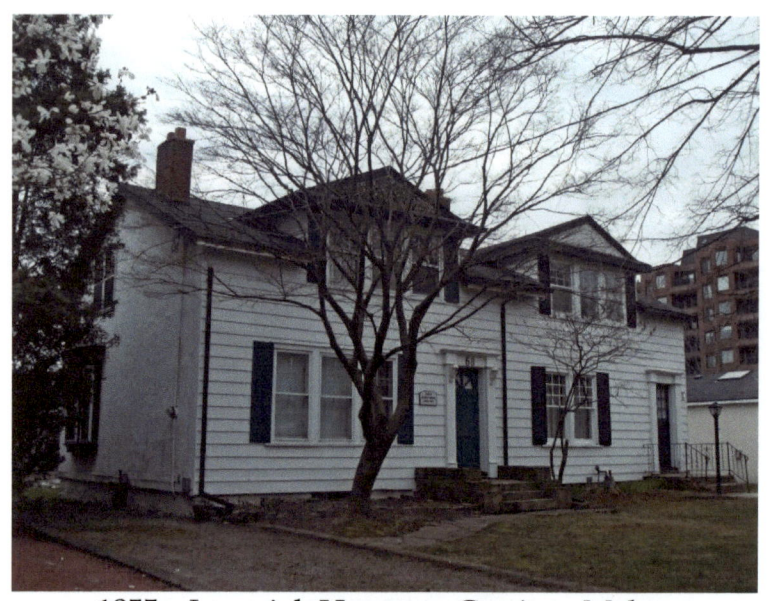

1855 – Jeremiah Hagman, Carriage Maker
68 Navy Street

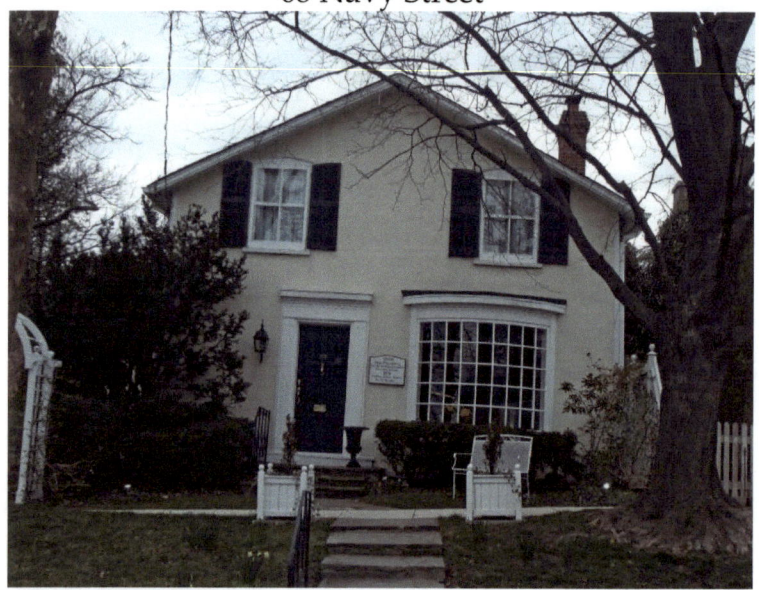

1828 – Ship's Chandlery established by William Chisholm,
Oakville's Founder – 115 Navy Street – Gothic Revival
1891 – Captain James Andrew, Yacht Builder

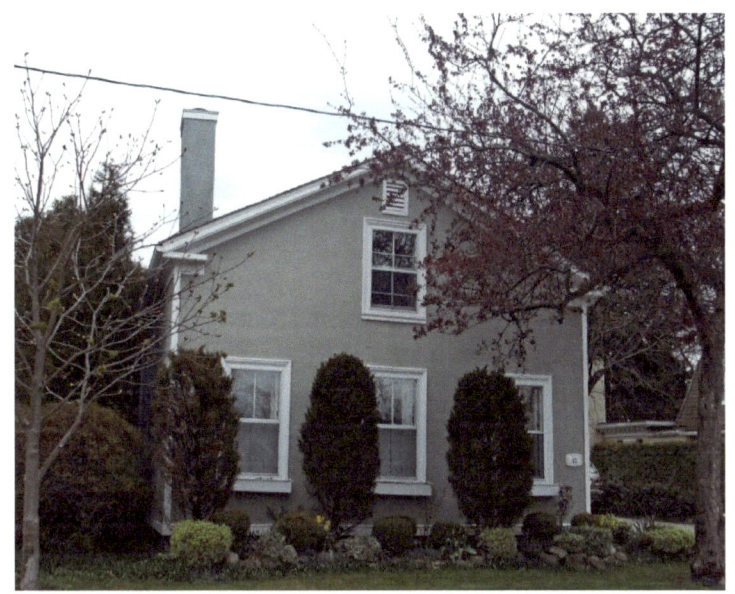

45 Navy Street – Gothic Revival, cornice return on gable

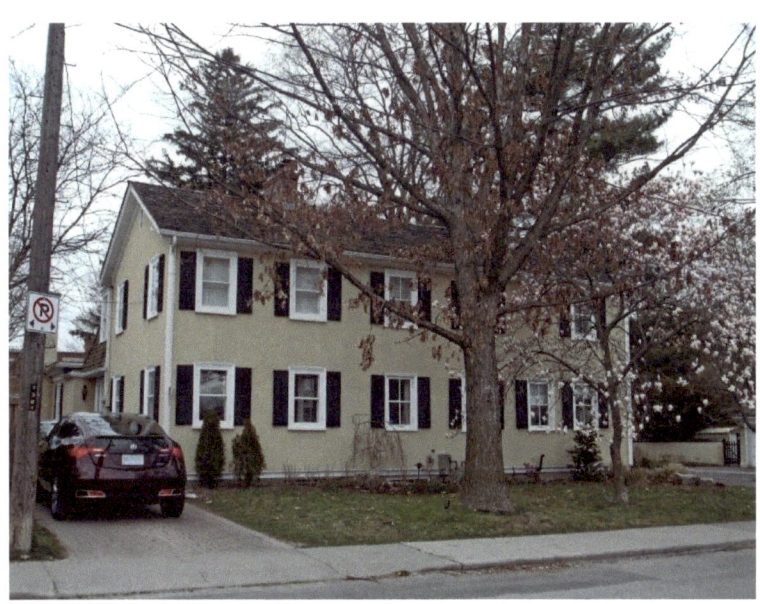

Georgian style

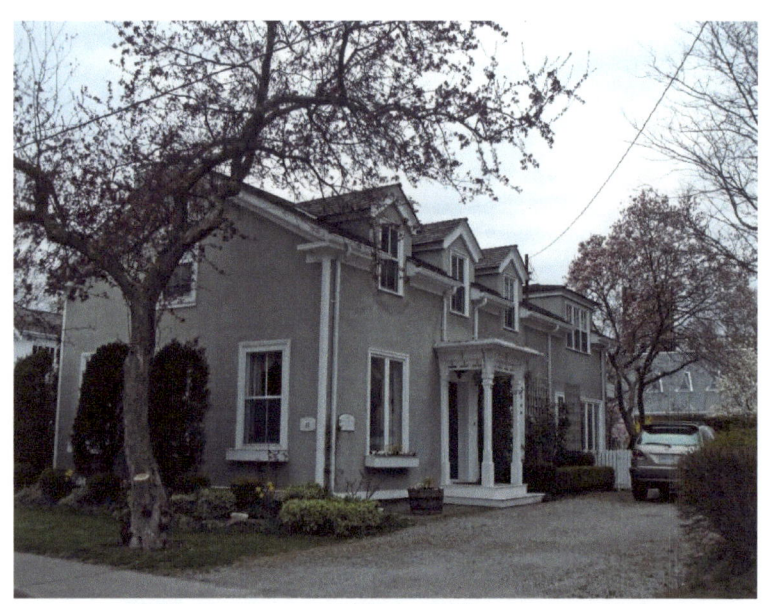

1830 Captain William Wilson, married
Moved to this site in 1859 - dormers

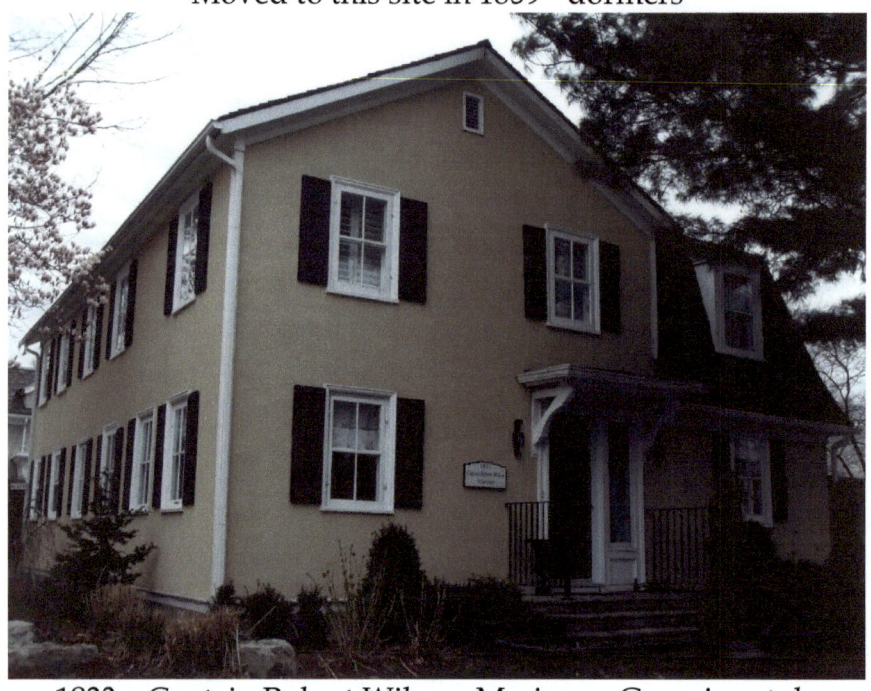

1833 – Captain Robert Wilson, Mariner – Georgian style

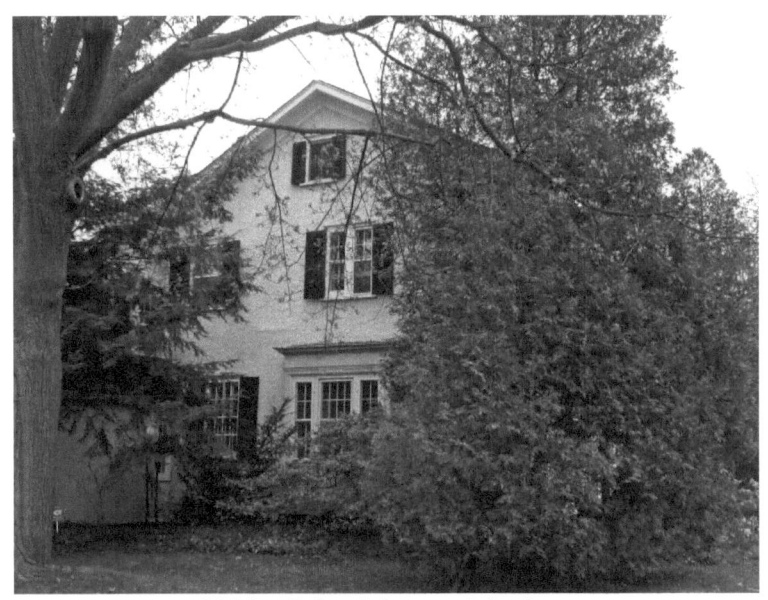

1838 – John Moore, Mariner
1853 – The Frontier House

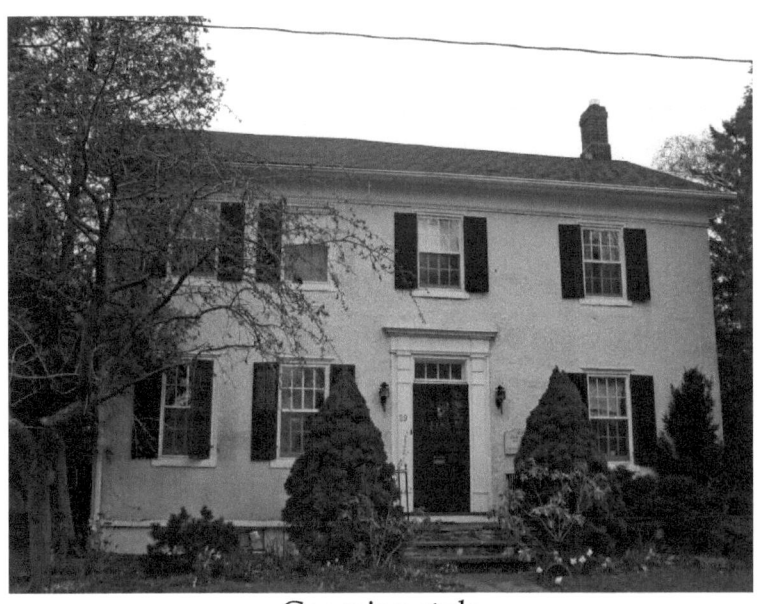

Georgian style

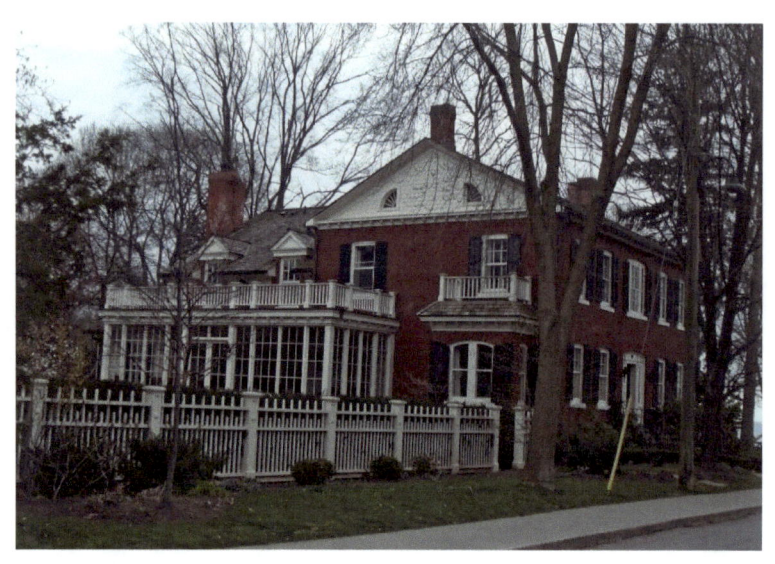

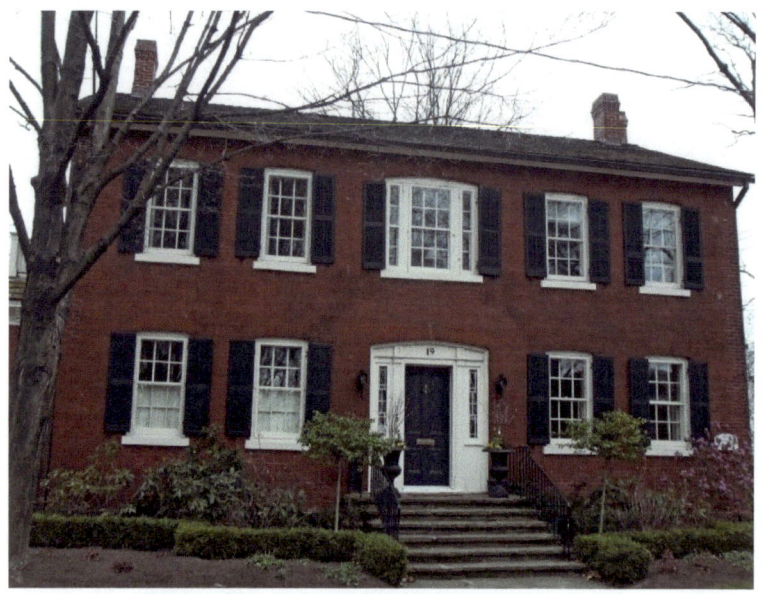

1835 – David Patterson, Shipbuilder
#19 - Georgian style

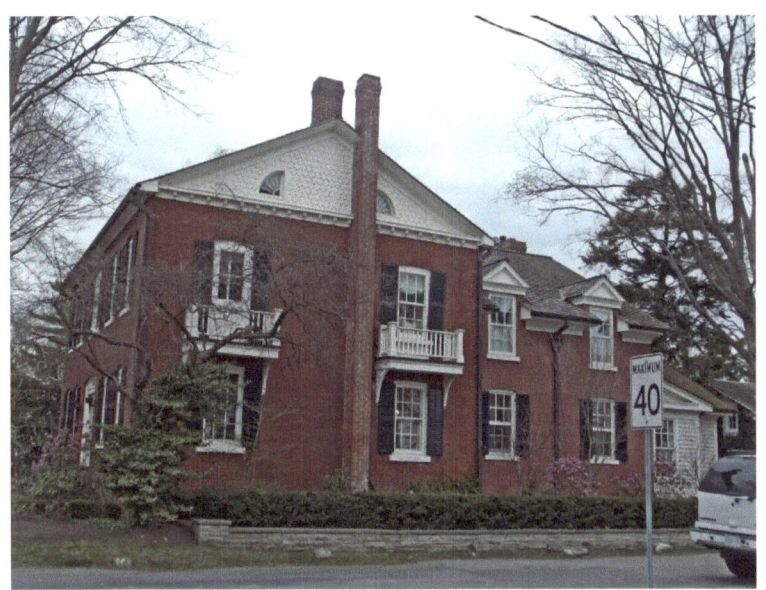

Gothic Revival, dormers

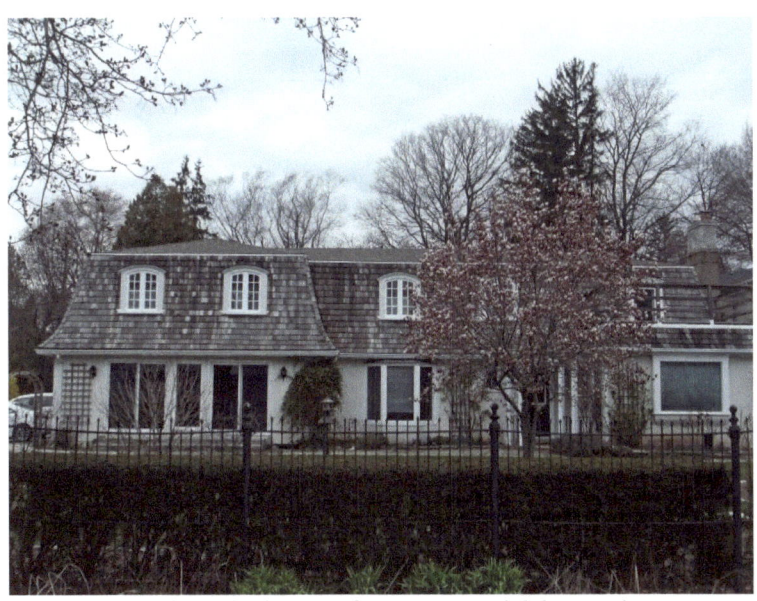

Cedar-shake roof – mansard-like style

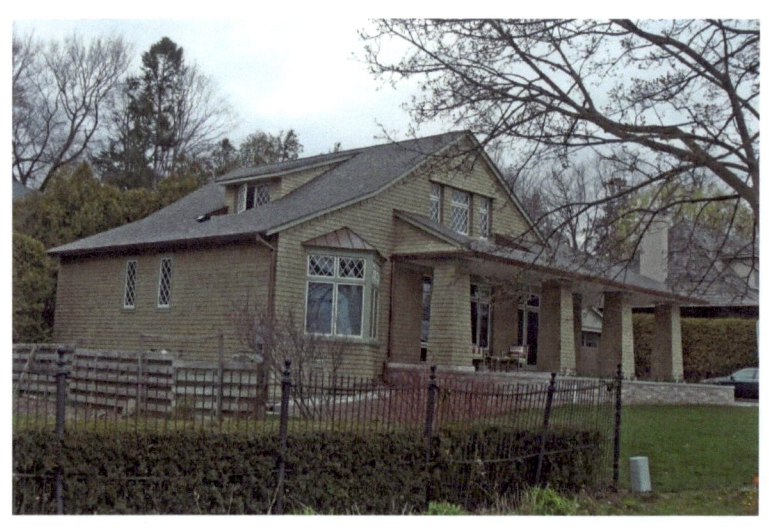

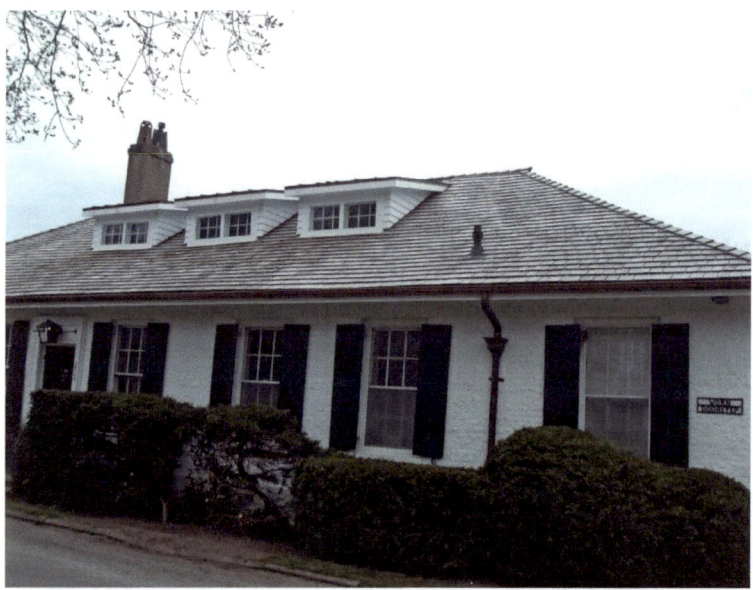

212 Front Street – cottage with gables

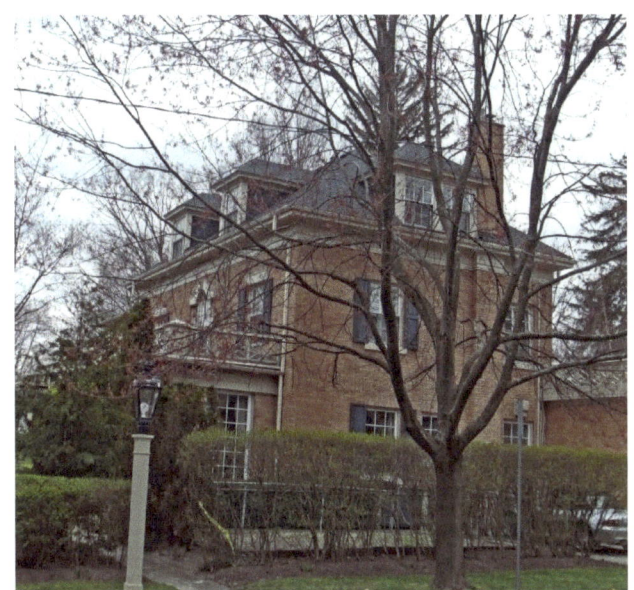

Italianate style, dormers

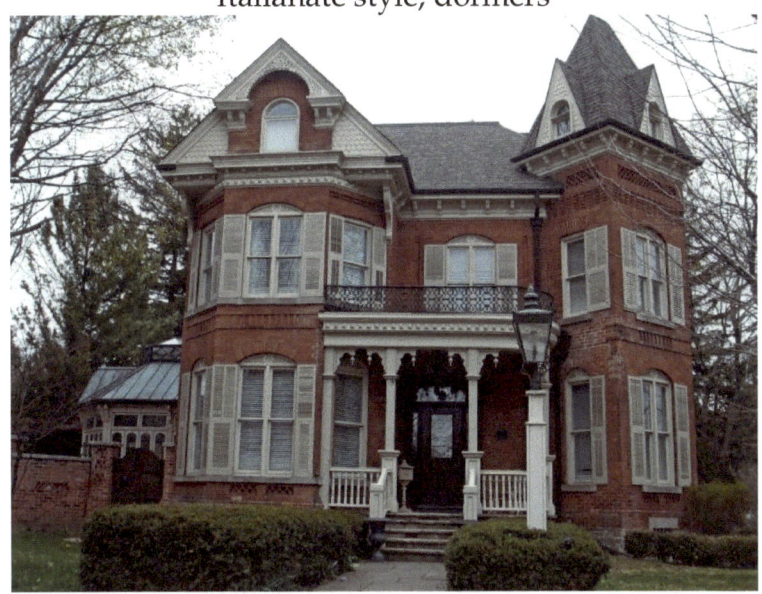

43 Dunn Street – Queen Anne style, towers, bay windows,
balcony on second floor, cornice brackets
Cecil Marlatt's estate

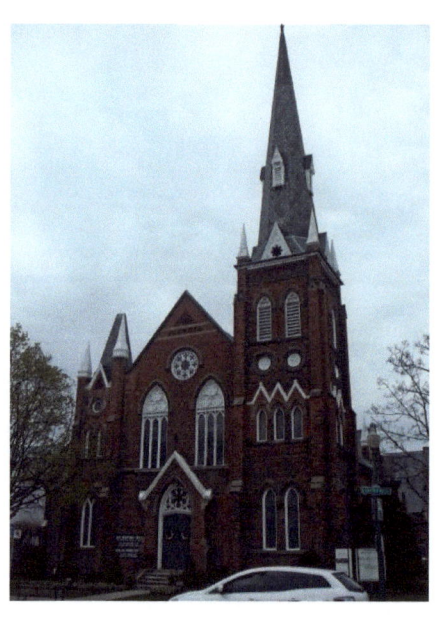

89 Dunn Street at Lakeshore Road -
Knox Presbyterian Church

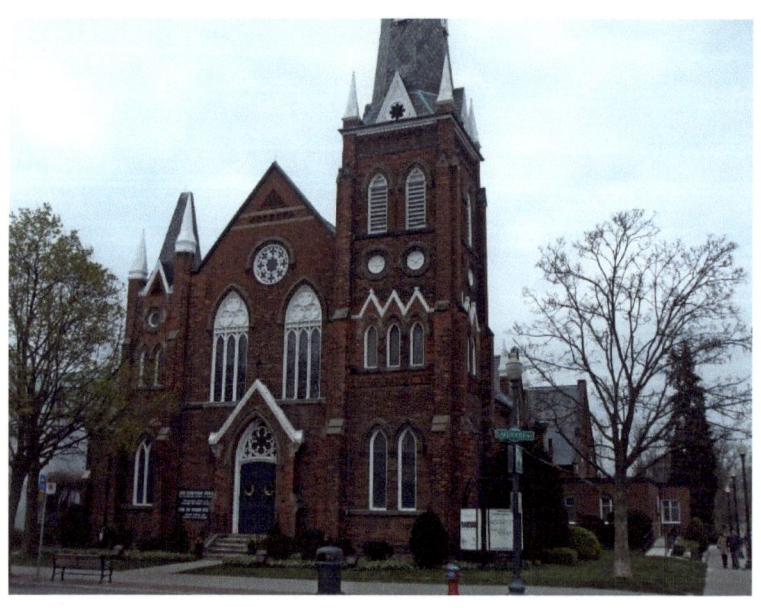

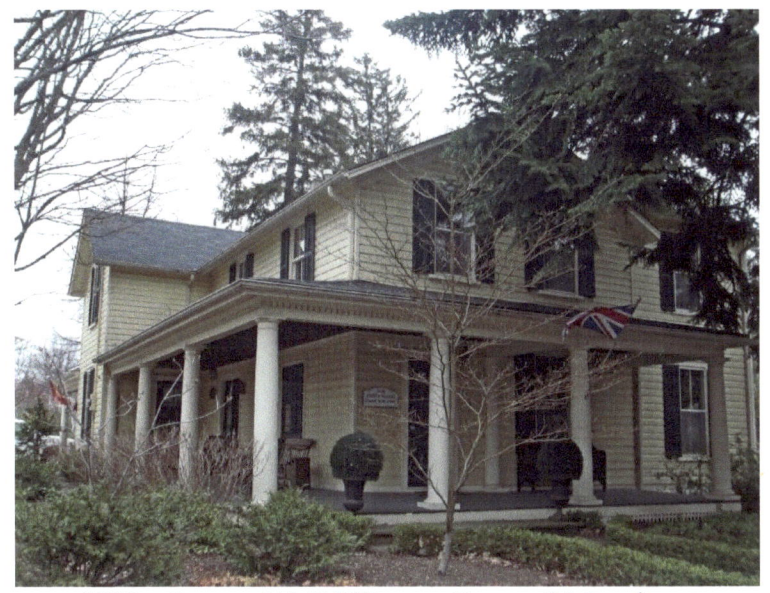

1838 – Justus W. Williams, General Merchant

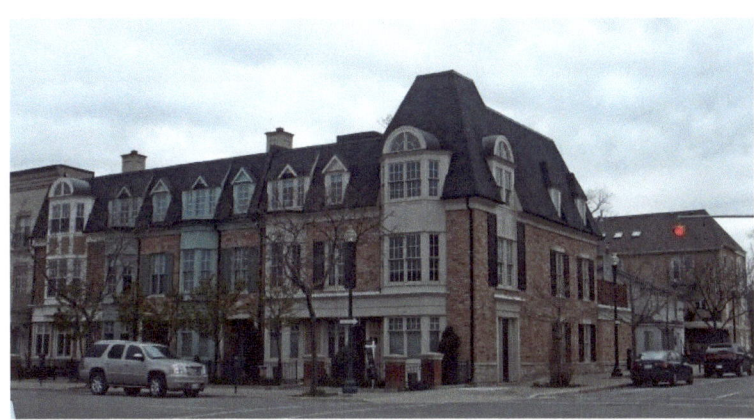

Downtown – Second Empire style, mansard roof, dormers

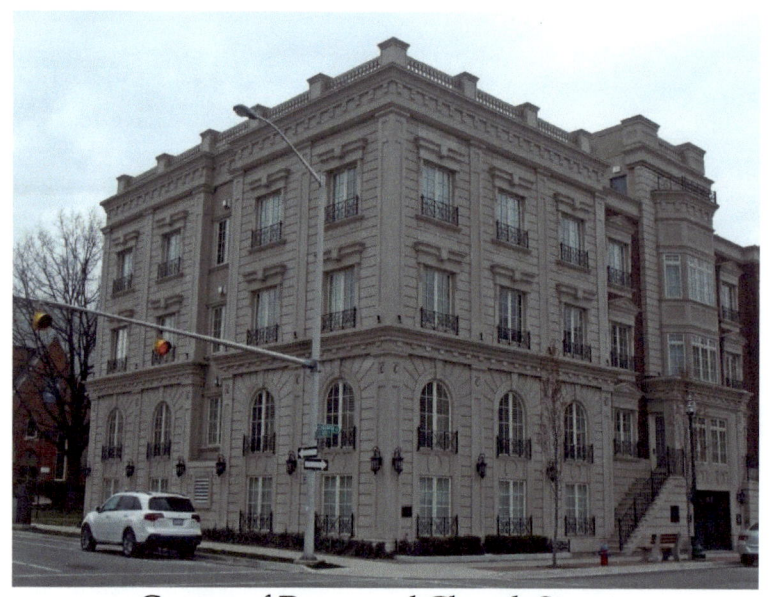

Corner of Dunn and Church Streets

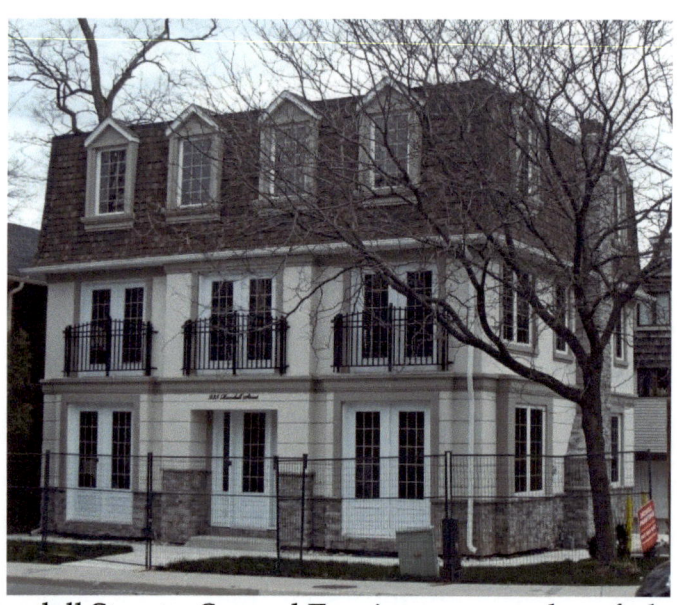

235 Randall Street – Second Empire - mansard roof, dormers

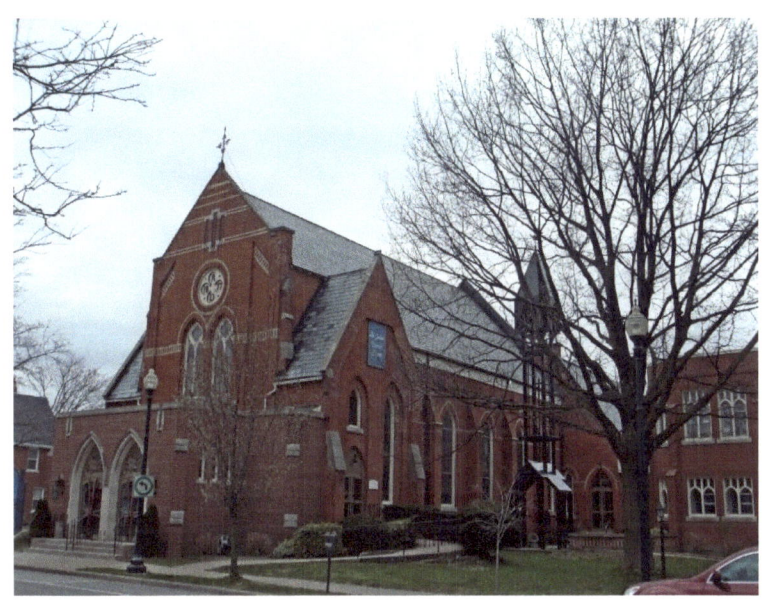

262 Randall Street – St. John's United Church
Established 1832 with Justus Wright Williams in attendance
brick building built 1877

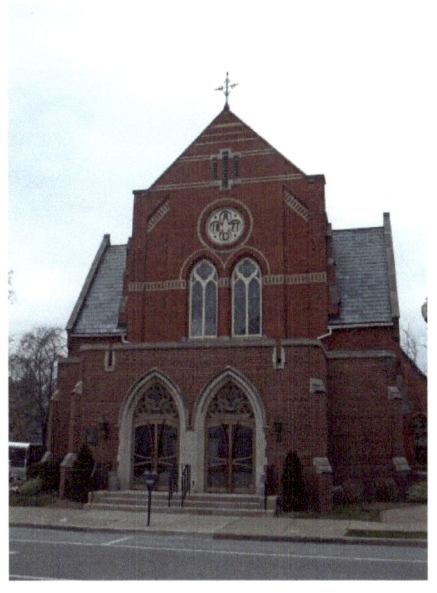

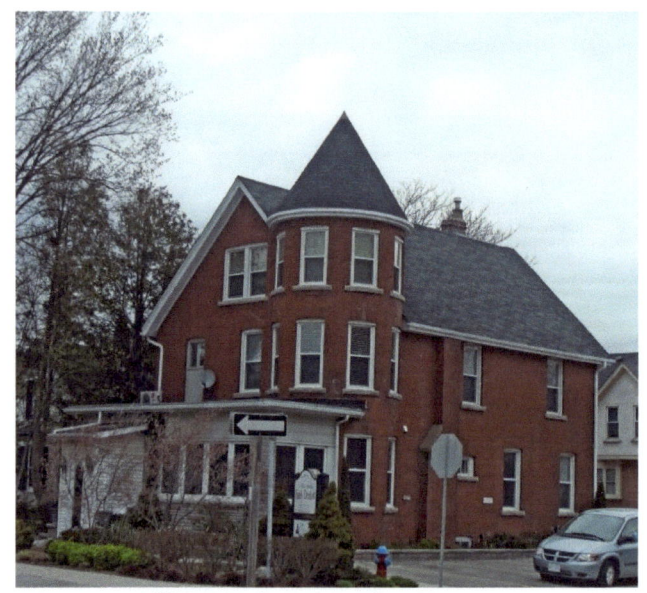

Queen Anne style - turret

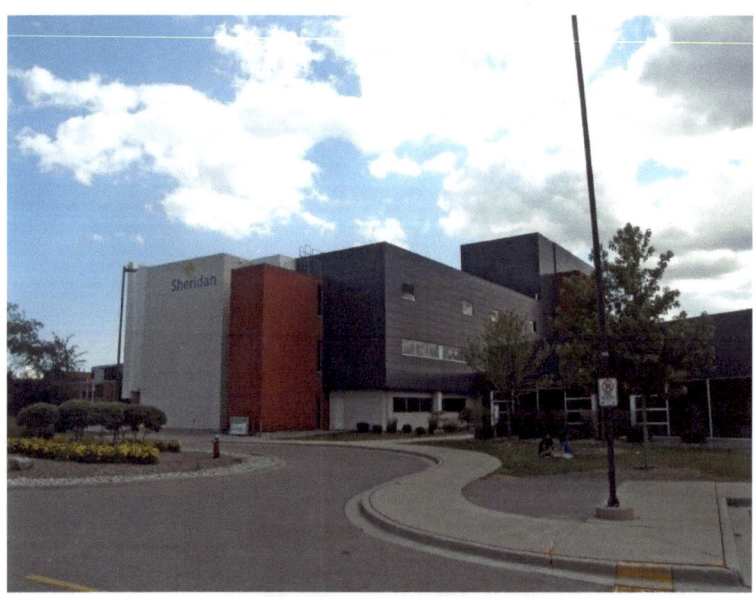

Sheridan College

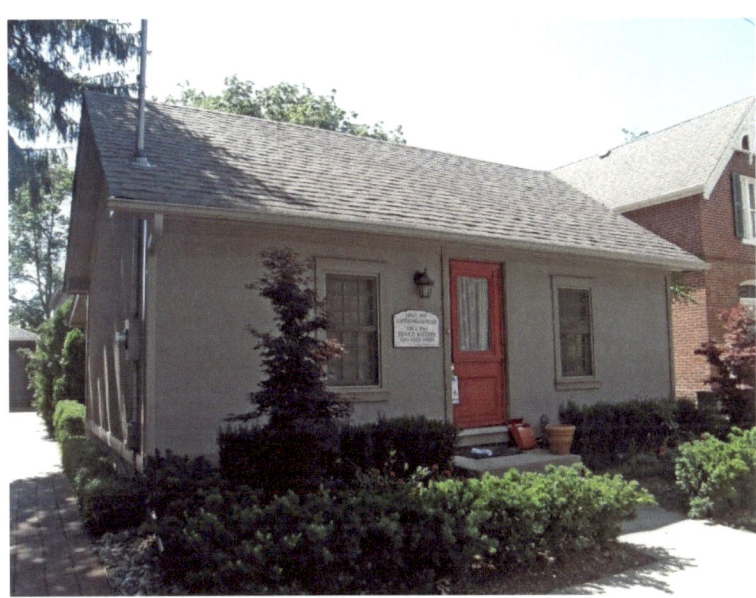

Circa 1849 – Captain William Wilson
Circa 1894 – Francis Matthews, Soda Water Works
Gothic Revival

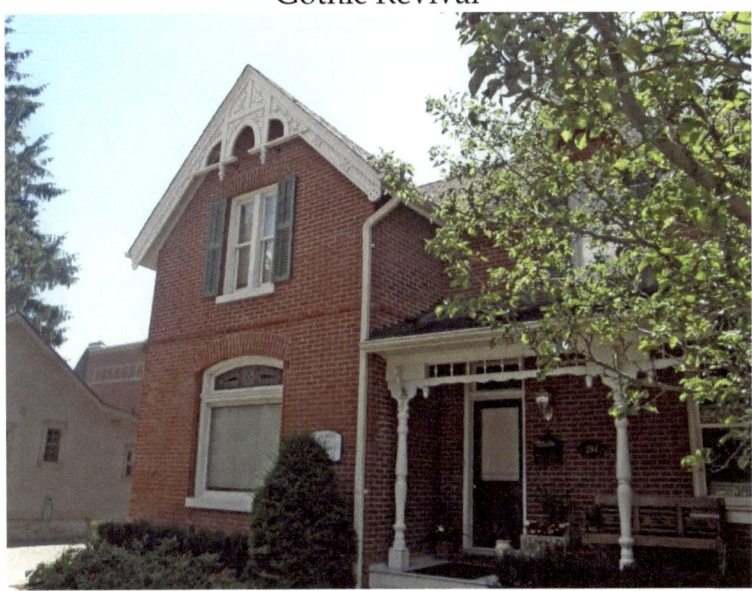

294 Sumner - circa 1870 – Captain William Wilson - two-storey
brick veneer house in Gothic style; verge board trim on gable

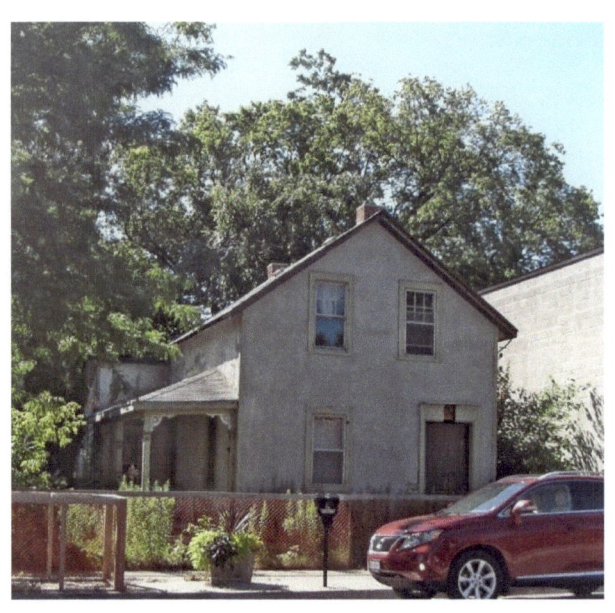

Gothic Revival

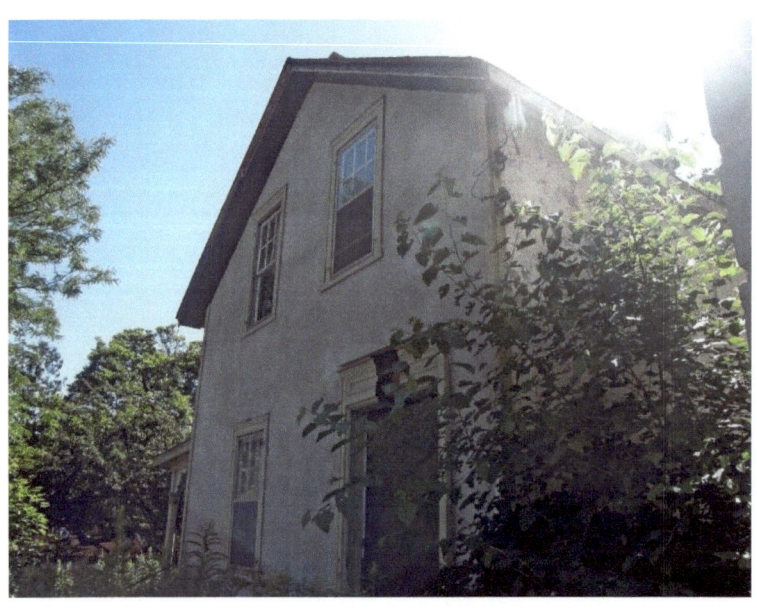

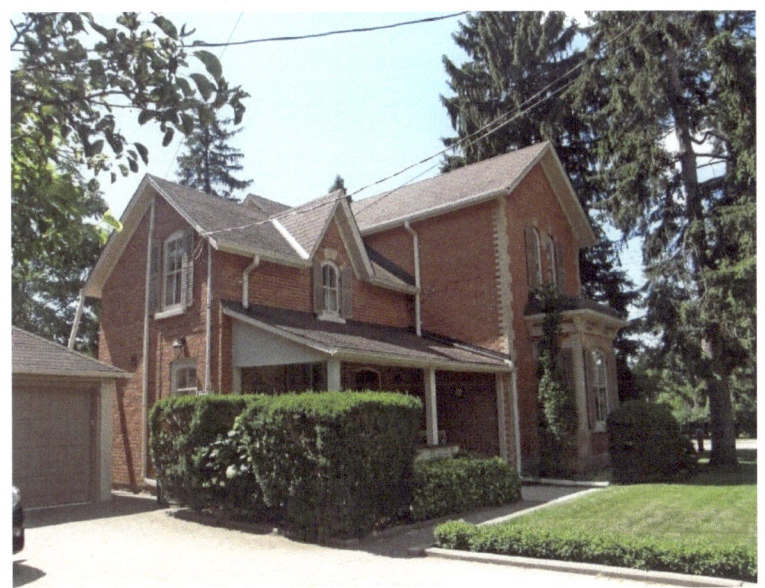

Corner quoins – Gothic Revival -

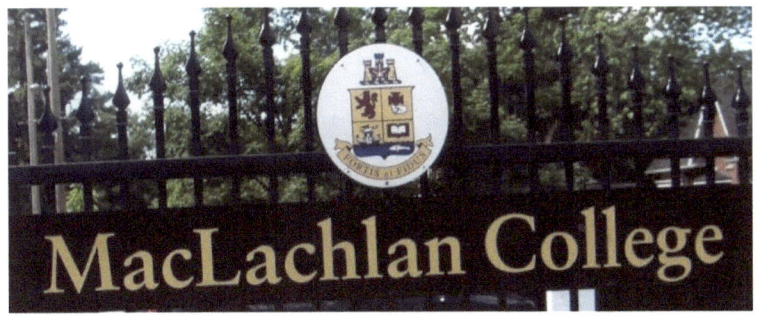

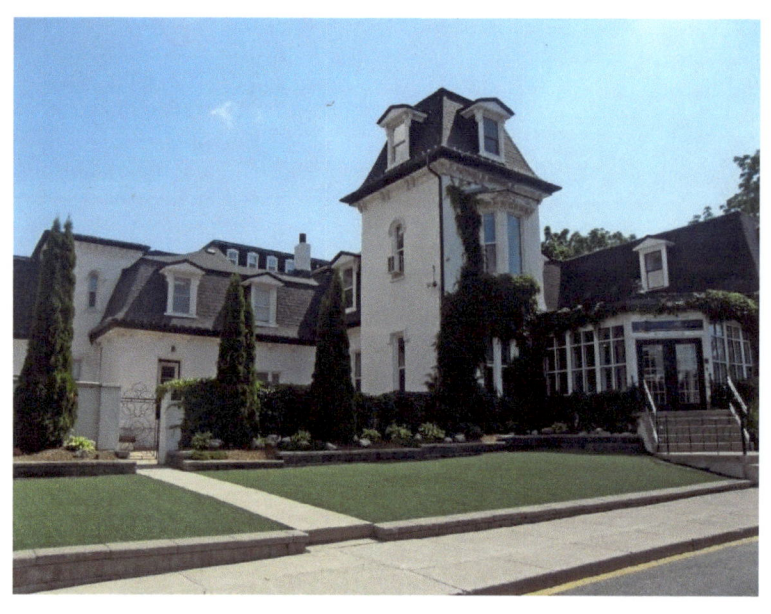

337 Trafalgar Road - MacLachlan College

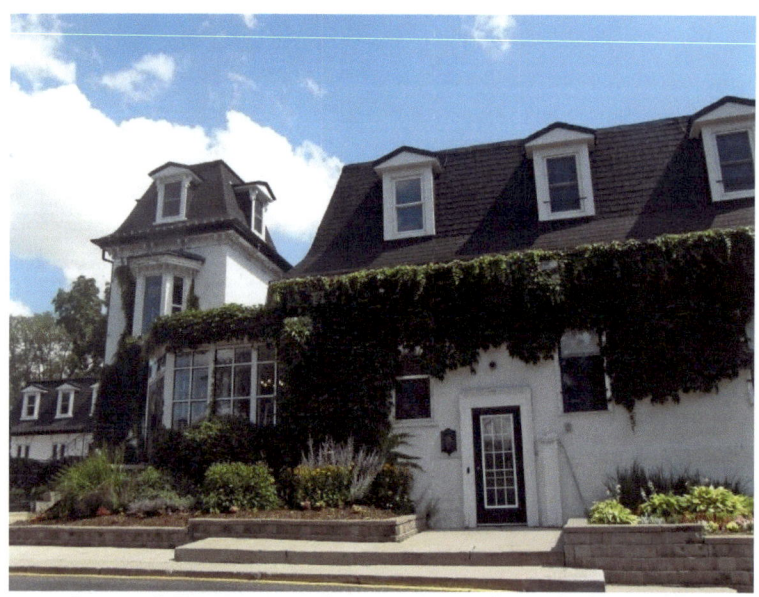

Second Empire style – mansard roof, dormers

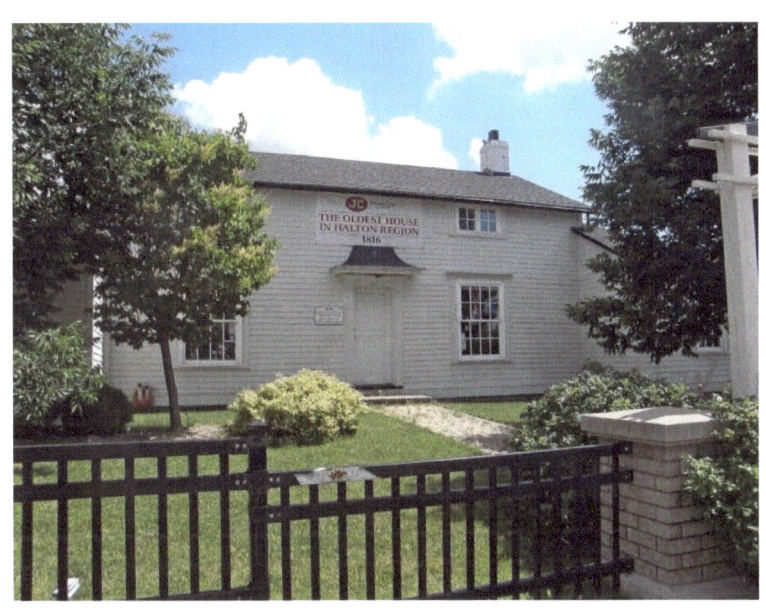

1816 – oldest house in Halton Region
Amos Biggar, United Empire Loyalist
Original Location: 502 Dundas Street West
Classic Revival style
Now The Cork House 2441 Neyagawa Boulevard

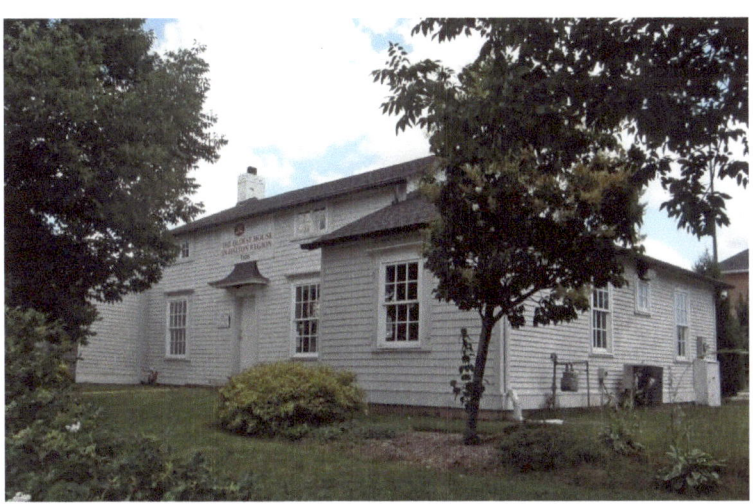

The Story of the Corkhouse

In 1808, before the town of Oakville existed, the Crown granted the land at 502 Dundas Street West to Daniel Shawson. In 1815, Mr. Shawson sold the land to a United Empire Loyalist named Amos Biggar. Biggar built the original rectangular section of this house in 1816. The house was built in the Classic Revival style, a good example of a Loyalist farmstead. Single storey additions were added to either side of the one-and-a-half storey original section; these additions were probably built by the next owner of the house, Philip Box. In 1853, the house was sold to Jonathan Pettit.

In 1903 the farm was sold to George King who reared at least nine children there. It was the childhood home of Dora King Cherrington (1906-1933). In 1936, the farm was sold to Harriet Pierce Bunting who in turn sold it to Taymouth Industries Limited in 1949.

In 2000 the home was moved to the corner of the property with the new address of 2441 Neyagawa Boulevard. The house is now home to Jelinek Cork Group and the Cork House.

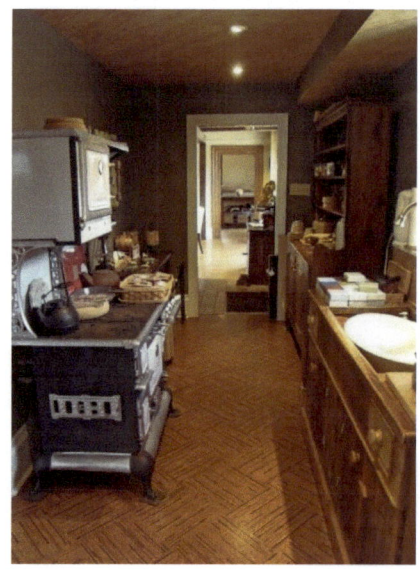

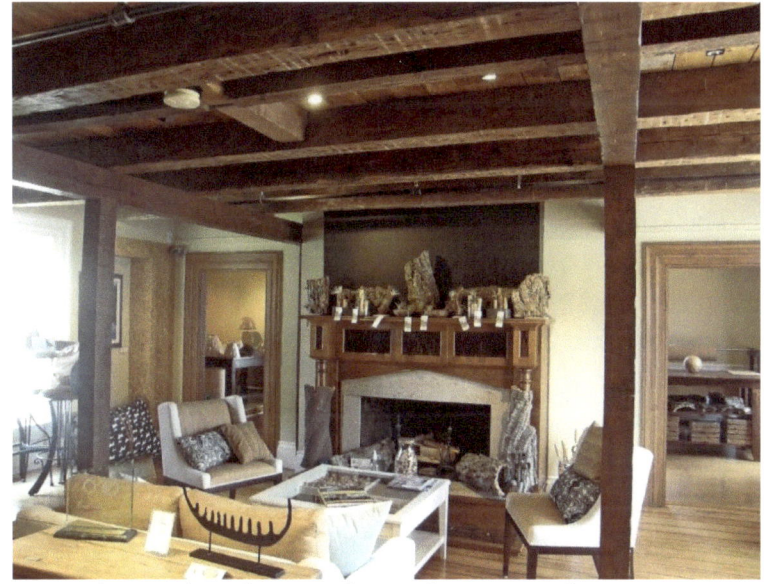

Wooden ceiling beams from the original construction

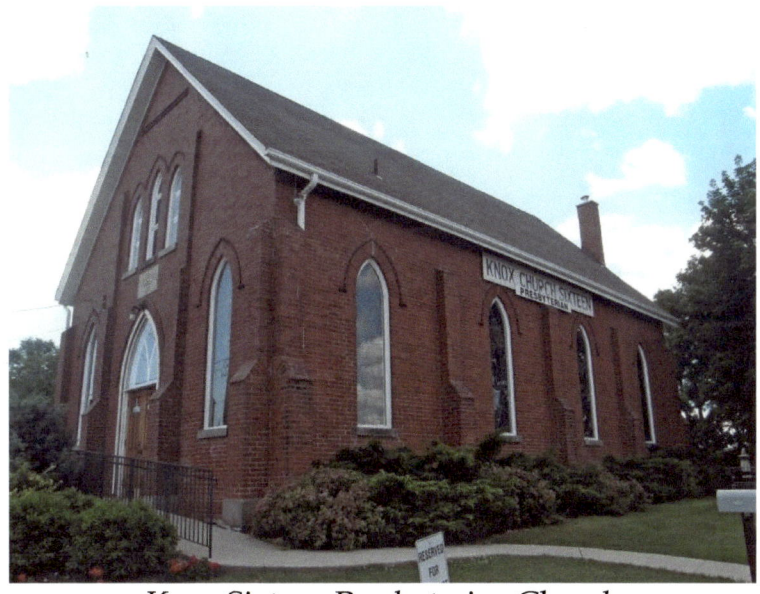

Knox Sixteen Presbyterian Church

Knox Sixteen Presbyterian Church is located on the east side of Sixteen Mile Creek just south of Dundas Street. It originally served the community of Sixteen Hollow. After that village declined, it continued to serve the surrounding farmers.

The congregation was organized in 1844. A wood frame structure was built the following year. The building was enlarged and bricked over in 1899. The church was lit by coal oil lambs until electric lights were installed in the 1940s.

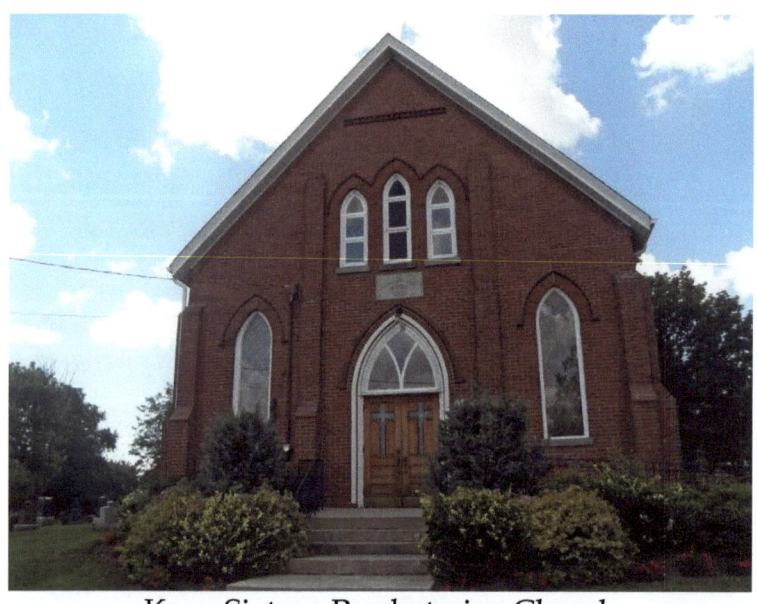

Knox Sixteen Presbyterian Church
First Service held 1844, church constructed 1846,
Brick exterior added 1899

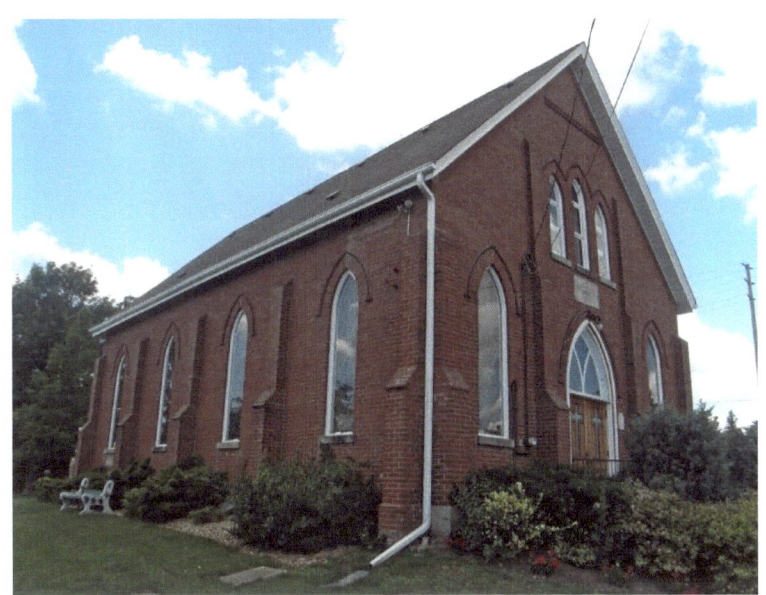

Buttresses, lancet windows

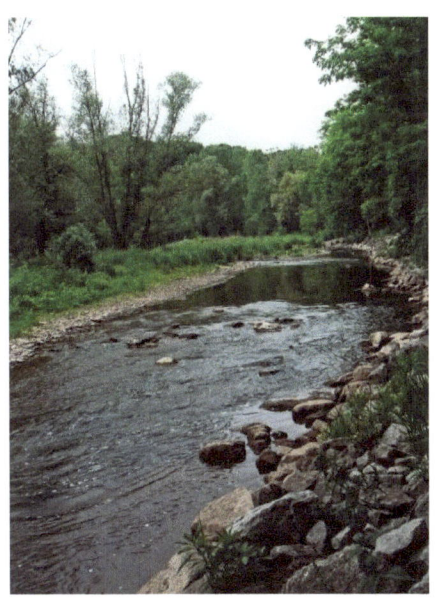

Modern buildings

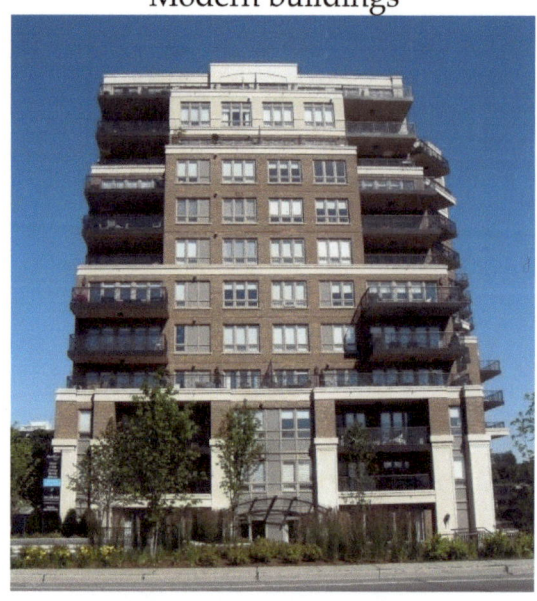

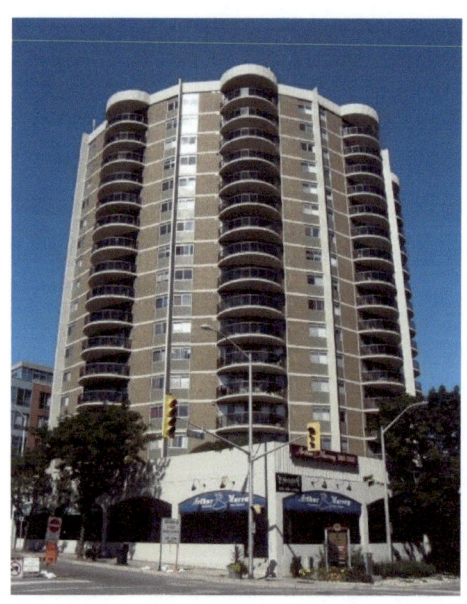

Architectural Terms

Brackets: a decorative or weight-bearing structural element which forms a right angle with one side against a wall and the other under a projecting surface such as an eave or roof. Example: 43 Dunn Street, Page 43	
Buttress: a masonry structure built against or projecting from a wall which serves to support or reinforce the wall. In Canadian architecture, they are sometimes used for decoration. Example: 160 William Street, Page 31	
Cornice Return: decorative element on the end of a gable. Example: Oakville Museum, see Page 23	
Dormer: (French for "sleep") a gable end window that pierces through the plane of a sloping roof surface to create usable space in the top floor or attic of a building by adding headroom. Example: 46 Burnet Street	
Gable: the triangular portion of a wall between the edges of a sloping roof. Example: see Page 46, Page 9	
Hipped Roof: a roof where all sides slope downwards to the walls with no gables. Example: 52 Burnet Street, Page 9	
Lancet Window: a tall, narrow window with a pointed arch at its top. Example: Knox Sixteen Presbyterian Church, Page 55	

Mansard Roof: This style was popularized by Francois Mansart (1598-1666), an accomplished architect of the French Baroque period and especially fashionable during the Second French Empire (1852-1870). This roof is almost flat on the top section, with two slopes on each of its sides with the lower slope at a steeper angle than the upper and having dormer windows. Example: 43 Burnet Street, Page 12	
Quoin: masonry blocks at the corner of a wall, often a decorative feature, usually larger or of a different colour than the rest of the wall. Example: 262 Randall Street, Page 47	
Rose Window: a circular window with ornamental tracery radiating from the centre. Example: St. Jude's Anglican Church, Page 28	
Turret: a small tower that projects from the wall of a building. Example: see Page 48	
Verge board and Finial: also called bargeboards – hang from the projecting end of a roof and are often elaborately carved and ornamented. **Finial:** ornament added to the top of a gable, pinnacle, canopy or spire – a Gothic element. Example: 294 Sumner, Page 45	

Building Styles

Georgian, before 1860 – This style began with the British King Georges in the 18th century. These buildings have balanced facades around a central door, medium-pitched gable roofs, and small paned windows. Example: see Page 33	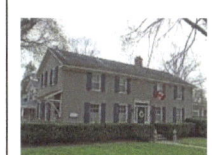
Gothic Revival, 1830-1890 – These decorative buildings have sharply-pitched gables with highly detailed verge boards, pointed-arch window openings, and dichromatic brickwork. It is a common style in Ontario. Example: 294 Sumner, Page 45	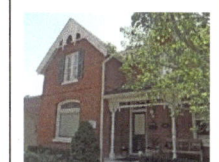
Italianate, 1850-1900 – It has wide-bracketed eaves, belvederes, wrap-around verandahs. Example: 52 Burnet Street, Page 9	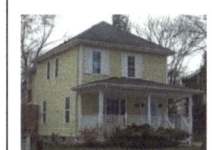
Queen Anne, 1885-1900 – This style is distinguished by an irregular outline featuring a combination of an offset tower, broad gables, projecting two-storey bays, verandahs, multi-sloped roofs, and tall, decorative chimneys. A mixture of brick and wood is common. Windows often have one large single-paned bottom sash and small panes in the upper sash. Example: 43 Dunn Street, Page 43	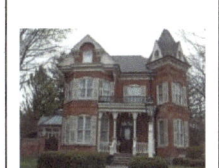
Second Empire, 1860-1880 – The mansard roof is the most noteworthy feature of this style and is evidence of the French origins. Projecting central towers and one or two-storey bays can also be present. Example: 235 Randall Street, Page 46	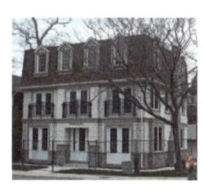

www.ingramcontent.com/pod-product-compliance
Lightning Source LLC
Chambersburg PA
CBHW040850180526
45159CB00001B/372